Jerry Levin's *West*  count to become a huma mation. The power of r oppression merges with solidarity with the victims, to produce a work of human affirmation that is at once compelling and disturbing. How the Israeli occupation translates itself into an intrusive and incessant source of pain for the ordinary Palestinian in Hebron is a moving tale and a glaring omission in media coverage and spin. Levin, and the Christian Peacemaker Teams, redefine the notion of endurance and heroism not only in the lives of the "ordinary" Palestinians but also in the nature of positive intervention and engagement that they themselves embody. – *Hanan Ashrawi*, Palestinian Legislative Council member and secretary general, The Palestinian Initiative for the Promotion of Global Dialogue and Democracy – MIFTAH.

These thoughtful and perceptive vignettes, written with sympathetic understanding and intimate knowledge, unveil the reality of life under military occupation, with its steady takeover of land and resources, and shattering of hopes for a decent existence. They are of inestimable value for anyone who hopes to comprehend what is taking place in the Middle East, and particularly so for Americans, whose footprint is everywhere and who have unparalleled opportunities to end oppression and violence and bring about a humane settlement. – *Noam Chomsky*

After decades of conflict, peace in the Middle East seems even more remote. Finally someone has shown the way. *West Bank Diary* by Jerry Levin offers unseen reports which lead to a dramatically new way to build peace. Out of the context of his own experience as a hostage he is able to bring convincing witness to the futility of all violence and he shows how "peacemaker teams" can bring new hope for all parties in the struggle. – *Thomas J. Gumbleton*, auxiliary bishop, archdiocese of Detroit, founder Pax Christ U.S.A.

Jerry Levin's reporting in *West Bank Diary* represents a challenge to mainstream media because of his being every day right where aggressive settler, army and police violence are taking place. His accounts are authentic. They are reporting with an experienced eye and ear for detail and facts developed during his years as an enterprising professional journalist with CNN. Also his captivity in 1984 as a hostage in Lebanon instilled in him a resolution to live nonviolently and a determination to see and speak about violence critically, which he has been doing ever since with great clarity.

The Christian message of peace permeates his diaries as well as other equally significant teachings concerning the need for coexistence of all religions and races in order to create a tolerant society here in Palestine and all of the Middle East. He highlights that need by including in every report descriptions of the frustration, ugliness, hatred, mean spirited brute force and passive acquiescence to it, as well as the powerlessness and pervasive sadness which he has observed while experiencing the occupations in Hebron, elsewhere in the West Bank and Baghdad.

His is a much needed new kind of reporting and analysis from the field where too much of what we think are facts are actually distortions or omissions filtered through smoke screens put up by journalists in the mainstream. Reading Levin's reports have inspired in me a determination to not just think – but rethink – my conclusions about how to tackle the profoundly troubling questions concerning war and peace in the world. *– Mordechai Vanunu,* *kidnapped from Rome by Israeli secret agents Sept. 30, 1986 who subsequently served 18 years in prison for revealing Israel's Dimona nuclear weapons facility secrets; elected rector of Glasgow University, Scotland, December 2004; in sanctuary at the Anglican St. George Cathedral, East Jerusalem since April 2004.*

Jerry Levin's book is a vital contribution to understanding the reality of the Holy Land – because of Mr. Levin's own high standards and level of achievement within international journalism, the depth of his experience in the Middle East and his consistency in providing his readers with that increasingly rare thing, actual News. *– Mark H. Andrus,* *bishop suffragan, Episcopal Diocese of Alabama*

A provocative, informative up-front set of literary "snap-shots" of the misery inflicted upon both Israelis and Palestinians by the continuing military occupation of the West Bank and the inevitable daily, often brutal and bloody, confrontations between the feared, frightened and hated soldiers of the IDF and the feared, frightened and hated Palestinian insurgents they try to control in and around Hebron. Written with sensitive discernment by a veteran journalist with long experience in the Middle East, this book is far more than political-military reporting on one of the most volatile flash points of the region. Jerry Levin has laid bare the moral, ethical, social struggles any honest, spiritually-searching person must undergo when faced with seemingly intractable conflict and unmistakable rights and wrongs on both sides. Not content with the role of detached commentator, Levin has committed himself to a prolonged period of service as a non-official observer at the sites of actual or potential violence, a silent witness for non-violence, justice and reconciliation. He writes of his self-imposed mission with modest self-effacement. It is hard to imagine a more courageous assignment in advocacy for peace. — *Landrum Bolling,* president emeritus of Earlham College, former rector of the Tantur Ecumenical Institute, Jerusalem

Jerry's story and his reflections really need to be heard as the tensions in the Middle East continue to escalate almost daily. He has lived through serious crises in many different situations and his reporting is always vivid and passionate, filled with real empathy for people and understanding of the big issues. At a time when terrorism is so much in the news, it's highly significant that he has looked terrorists in the face and knows how their minds work. And because he has moved from a position of no faith to a deeply-held Christian faith, his writing will strike a chord with people of all faiths — and of none. These pieces provide an inspired commentary on some of the crucial events in the region that have been unfolding before our eyes. — *Colin Chapman,* former lecturer in Islamic studies, Near East School of Theology, Beirut and author of Whose Promised Land? and Whose Holy City? Jerusalem and the Israeli-Palestinian Conflict.

Jerry Levin uses nonviolent methods in the most practical way by being a volunteer with the Christian Peacemaker Teams, involving himself with the people surrounding him and putting his commitment to peace by addressing the tough issue of reducing violence between the Palestinians and the Israelis. Jerry and his wife Sis became a voice from the inside bringing their message to the outside world for action and personal testimony. His reports show a deep care and compassion for all humans and especially those who are being deprived of their human and civil rights. Jerry sees the suffering from the victim's side as well as the victimizer's and he writes about it for all of us to be better able to understand the tragedy people are living in day by day. *Mubarak Awad, Nonviolence International, Jerusalem*

Levin's book shouldn't be the only one you read about the Middle East. But if you're curious why peace eludes the region and imagine, along with most supporters of Israel, that all would be fine "if the Palestinians would just leave us alone," here's a good chance to find out what your friends over there aren't telling you and the media doesn't find newsworthy. Levin's devastating eyewitness report of daily oppression by Israeli occupation forces, civilian and military, is not fun reading, but after 38 years of constant, systematic human-rights violations, perhaps it's time for all those genuinely concerned with the glorious legacy of Jewish morality and compassion to graduate from a blissful ignorance into an informed activism for a just peace between Israelis and Palestinians. This book will surely help in this effort.

It's an angry book, and I think that should be mentioned, something to the effect of, "witnessing what he's seen would put anyone's belief in nonviolence to the test." Jerry Levin gets mighty angry, softening only in his moving interview of Mordecai Vanunu with whom he so closely identifies, but he doesn't lose his faith. —*Rabbi Jeremy Milgrom, founder, Rabbis For Human Rights*

Jerry Levin's *West Bank Diary* is a lucid, direct and stimulating account of his firsthand experiences in the Palestinian West Bank, Israel and Iraq. In this compendium of his periodic circulars, "From the Inside Looking Out," he reflects vividly on the effects of violence and nonviolence on the people he observed, inter viewed and lived with in the Middle East. Jerry captures strikingly the tragic consequences of the military occupation and the violence it creates. His experience working with the Christian Peacemaker Teams in Hebron, his commitment for a just peace through nonviolence and his journalistic professionalism enable him not only to analyze the situation of oppression but also to draw out insightful conclusions that assist the reader in feeling and understanding the predicament of all those caught in the web of the Israeli military occupation. The *West Bank Diary* is an eye-opener for those who want to see and comprehend the human tragedy from the pen of a veteran journalist. – *The Rev. Dr.* **Naim Ateek**, *director, Sabeel Ecumenical Liberation Theology Center, Jerusalem*

Having followed many of Jerry Levin's regular dispatches, "From the Inside Looking Out" in recent years, one is struck by the sheer weight of the occupation and its assault on the dignity of both the Palestinian civilians and the dehumanizing effects on the Israeli soldiers. Jerry's insights and the courageous and creative nonviolent engagement of the Christian Peacemaker Teams leave the reader with insights not readily available from the bland and usually naïve accounts in the Western media. Jerry's personal journey as a hard-core secular Jewish journalist and Beirut hostage to Christian peacemaker to enlistment as a compassionate Christian witness living in the "eye of the storm" of the Israeli occupation is itself a testimony to the power of reconciliation based on authentic justice. If true prophecy is having one's eyes and ears attuned to God's Kingdom, where the poor are to be blessed and the peacemakers are the children of God, then this account is truly a prophetic account of the tragedy unfolding in the Holy Land today. – *Rev. Dr.* **Donald E. Wagner**, *Professor and Director of the Center for Middle Eastern Studies at North Park University, Chicago*

At age 70 after a brilliant career as a journalist, Jerry Levin joined Christian Peacemaker Teams as a full-time worker. Since then he has spent much of his time in Palestine, Israel and Iraq getting in the way of violence and documenting the sources and conditions of violence. His journalist eye has helped all of us see beyond the immediate crisis that our teams may be facing. Readers will soon sense that he is a marvelous coworker, engaging speaker and competent analyst with his feet firmly planted on the ground. This book began as an occasional posting on a list serve: "From the Inside Looking Out." By stretching to combine the personal, the spiritual and the political, Jerry has built up a large support network that includes seekers, new converts to the world of international affairs and seasoned participants with various perspectives. If anyone can speak from the "inside" to give all of us a fresh look that allows us to breathe, Jerry can. His writing creates the conditions for all the contending forces to be "warmed by the light of God." – *Gene Stolzfus*, founding director, Christian Peacemaker Teams

Jerry Levin's *West Bank Diary* is an impassioned witness to the struggle of Palestinians and a detailed look at the many methods by which Israel maintains and expands its oppressive occupation. Levin's reports, which reflect his passion for truth as well as his commitment to justice and peace, recall the Biblical passage from Zechariah: "With truth, with peace and with justice, judge in your gates." Jerry's rare combination of a reporter's eye and ear for detail and a human rights/peace worker's compassion for people results in this remarkable set of reports – which are at times too painful to read. Jerry – and others – have made it clear that Israel continues its nearly 60-year pattern of expelling the indigenous Palestinians. Witnessing this history is necessary, but not sufficient. As Thoreau noted: "It takes two to speak the truth: one to speak, and another to hear." What is now necessary is for those who understand the truth to convince the American people and government to insist on justice and peace in Palestine/Israel. – *Ned Hanauer*, director, Search for Justice and Equality in Palestine/Israel, Framingham, MA

Jerry Levin's book is an important contribution to those who seek Middle East peace. If only every American and every Israeli were to read this book, it would have a profound impact in providing the kind of experiential on-the-ground knowledge that the media rarely gives us, and would provide a basis for a new politics based on open-heartedness and generosity rather than on triumphalism and hoping that one side will ultimately *win*.

The Christian Peacemakers Team which Levin joined in Hebron is doing remarkable work, and I can only pray that more people with this level of courage will become non-violent observers of the reality, thereby transforming that reality. – *Rabbi Michael Lerner*, *author of* Healing Israel/Palestine *and editor,* Tikkun Magazine, A Bimonthly Jewish and Interfaith Critique of Politics, Culture and Society

Jerry Levin can plant seeds of hope in an apparently hopeless situation because of his indomitable faith. Through powerful stories, his *West Bank Diary* evokes Palestinians' day-to-day struggle to survive under a military occupation. Equally inspiring is Jerry Levin's own pilgrimage into the inner fires of Christian nonviolence, as a member of an heroic Christian Peacemakers Team in Hebron. If you were privileged to read Sis Levin's *Beirut Diary,* you already know Sis and Jerry's transforming story of his God-given liberation from captivity as a hostage in Lebanon. Here, then, is the Spirit-linked sequel – a diary of the life of nonviolence born from that Beirut epiphany. The story continues, widens and deepens. This Levin in the leaven of Palestine means hope. – *Jim Douglass, author and peace activist*

Jerry Levin is a man who has the courage to change his mind when he encounters new truth. We will have to ask his critics (and there will be some) whether they have the same courage. – *John K. Stoner, coördinator, Every Church A Peace Church*

Jerry Levin's subject matter is counter-intuitive or at least un-fashionable, which makes it all the more important. Moreover, Levin's prose style is unfailingly riveting. I have never been able to put one single report of his down – they just captivate the reader's attention! His moral weight plus his credibility as a former hostage in Lebanon and his piercing, affecting and sometimes also ironic accounts of what he has seen and heard in the Middle East: these qualities make this book memorable and a definite must Read. – *The Very Rev. Dr. Theol. Paul F. M. Zahl*, dean and president, *Trinity Episcopal School for Ministry, Ambridge, PA*

WEST BANK
DIARY

WEST BANK DIARY

Middle East Violence as Reported
by a Former American Hostage

Jerry Levin

Hope Publishing House
Pasadena, California

For information address:

Hope Publishing House
P.O. Box 60008
Pasadena, CA 91116 - U.S.A.
Tel: (626) 792-6123 / Fax: (626) 792-2121
E-mail: hopepub@sbcglobal.net
Web site: http://www.hope-pub.com

Printed on acid-free paper
Cover design — Michael McClary/The Workshop

Library of Congress Cataloging-in-Publication Data

Levin, Jerry.
    West Bank diary : Middle East violence as reported by a former
American hostage / Jerry Levin ; introduction by Landrum R. Bolling. --
1st. American pbk. ed.
        p. cm.
    ISBN-10: 1-932717-03-X (pbk. : alk. paper)
    ISBN-13: 978-1-932717-03-7
    1. Hebron--Description and travel. 2. Levin, Jerry--Diaries. 3. West
Bank--Description and travel. 4. Palestinian Arabs--West Bank--Hebron.
5. Arab-Israeli conflict--1993- 6. Violence--Middle East. I. Title.
    DS110.H4L485 2005
    956.95'3044--dc22
                        2005003776

This collection is dedicated to

The late Mazen Dana, a creative Palestinian photojournalist and long-time friend to Christian Peacemaker Teams. In the course of covering without flinching the occupation of Palestine, the much honored newsman was beaten and wounded more than once by Israeli soldiers and border police only to be shot to death in August 2003 by American soldiers covering another occupation, this time in Iraq. He was killed while videotaping outside the Abu Ghraib prison.

and to

Hazem Bader, the still very much alive and filming Palestinian photojournalist. In the spring of 2005 I came across him being physically harassed by an Israeli soldier who objected to his taking pictures of young men being detained at the Beit Romano checkpoint leading into Hebron's Old City. The soldier gun in hand was screaming "Give me your camera! Give me your camera!" while trying to rip it from Bader's hands. Pushing the soldier's gun gently away, the veteran of many such encounters said quietly and calmly and without flinching, "Give me your gun and I'll give you my camera." Soon the soldier backed off, gun still in hand but without the camera.

Contents

Introduction, *Landrum R. Bolling* ix
Prologue xiii
Acknowledgments xvii

PALESTINE – *July 2002 – January 2003*

1. Sometimes I Think Everything Is Area Z 1
2. Our God Will Kill Your God! 5
3. The Settlers Are Angry 9
4. Looking for the Big Fish 16
5. Have a Nice Day 21
6. School Daze in Hebron–Part 1 25
7. School Daze in Hebron–Part 2 30
8. There Goes the Neighborhood 35
9. Nights of the Furies 40
10. Road Rage 44
11. The Dying Stones 48
12. Supposing Everything West of the Mississippi Was
    Palestine 52

IRAQ/JORDAN – *March 2003 – June 2003*

13. Trusting God More and Our Military Less 56
14. Who Is Babylon? 60
15. Where Have All the Lovebirds Gone? 64
16. Robbing the Cradle 68
17. Bush Broke it. Why Doesn't He Fix it? 71
18. A Tank Called "Hostile" 76
19. Questions and Some Answers 82

20. Waiting for Garner 88
21. Will the Real Ali Baba Please Stand up? 94
22. These Things Take Time 98

PALESTINE – *July 2003 – January 2005*

23. While You Were Gone 102
24. Catch-22s in the Land of Milk and Honey 106
25. The Baladyeh and the Baptismal Font–Part 1 110
26. The Baladyeh and the Baptismal Font–Part 2 115
27. The Baladyeh and the Baptismal Font–Part 3 119
28. While You Were Gone–Episode 2 125
29. "Mirror, Mirror on the Wall" 130
30. We Get Letters 133
31. Bad Fences Don't Make Good Neighbors 137
32. Seeing the Forest as Well as the Trees 142
33. The Sad Sounds of Silence 146
34. "Now the Sun Sets at 2:30" 152
35. Only Half the Story 156
36. Which Came First? 161
37. "Piece Process" Update 165
38. While You Were Gone–Episode 3 169
39. Remembrance of Horrors Past and Present –
    Iraq 2004/Lebanon 1984 173
40. CTSD! 177
41. CTSD!–Part 2 181
42. CTSD!–Part 3 185
43. Seasons Greetings 190
44. Mordechai 192
45. Mordechai Vanunu's Not-so-excellent Christmas Eve
    Adventure 197
46. Mordechai and the Double Standard 202
47. Mordechai Vanunu's Interview–CONTINUED 207
    Epilogue 212

Introduction

Landrum R. Bolling
DIRECTOR-AT-LARGE, MERCY CORP

In the interest of transparency and full disclosure, let me say straightaway that I am a long-time admirer and personal friend of Jerry Levin and his wife Sis. With them I share a deep concern for a fair and just resolution of the Israeli/Palestinian conflict, a concern that has intensified during the many years we have lived and worked in the region. With them I affirm a common sense of appreciation for the fine human qualities, extraordinary talents, soaring hopes and ambitions of the two embattled peoples.

It is possible and essential to be both pro-Israeli and pro-Palestinian—and at the same time to be a sensitive, responsible truth-teller about the horrible acts of destructive cruelty each side has committed against the other. Jerry is remarkably equipped and positioned to be such a speaker of truth.

It is important, of course, to have credible witnesses to the horrible stories of the rights and wrongs of this prolonged, bitter Middle-East struggle. We need to know the facts, but it is even more important to hear the observations and reflections of informed observers who can go beyond the sensationalism of the gory events of the moment to articulate with thoughtful discernment the emerging, disturbing realities about the role of violence in this turbulent era. We must be forcefully reminded of the monstrous consequences of violence for both peoples and its ultimately hopeless futility. This book is such a reminder.

Violence is not the way to settle disputes. Violence breeds more violence. Terror produces counter-terror which produces more terror. Tit-for-tat reprisals get us nowhere except to more misery for more people. Yet the right of reprisal appears, to this day, to be one of the most highly prized "rights" many people in all cultures and leaders in most governments stubbornly cling to. Every person and every nation, we say, has the "right of self-defense." That has come to mean not only the right to retaliate after an attack but, for some, even the right to make a preëmptive strike to prevent what somebody thinks might be an imminent attack.

Every victim, we say, has the right to "justice" – by which we often mean prompt and severe punishment of those labeled as attackers – as a way of providing necessary compensation for the victims of attack. Yet where does all this stop? When and how does one determine whether the accounts have been squared so that nobody "needs" further compensating revenge?

Most of us don't have to wrestle with that kind of question on the personal level. We have the luxury of debating the pros and cons of such issues as matters of abstract philosophical principle or as problems in national military and foreign-affairs policy. Jerry Levin has come to terms with these issues on a different and very personal basis.

As the Middle East bureau chief for the television news network CNN in the 1980s, Jerry witnessed and reported on the civil war in Lebanon from up-close. In that role he demonstrated professional objectivity, fairness and humane concern. He did not rush to judgment and demonize one faction or another – or all. In no way could he have been considered an enemy of any group.

Nevertheless, he was snatched off the street in Beirut as he walked to work one early morning, shoved on to the floor of a car, blindfolded and hustled off to solitary confinement in a hillside house in the Beqaa Valley. As the hostage of a radical Islamic group determined to force changes in the region, Jerry was for eleven-and-a-half months isolated from the world, surrounded by armed guards with whom he had no common language and whose faces he was not allowed to see.

There, in that hostile environment, he began an extended spiritual journey that led him from the secular atheism of his Jewish parents who had lost their faith to a clear and inspiring faith in a God of love and reconciliation. Along the way, he managed to persuade his captors to bring him a Bible. He had never read the Bible, either the Hebrew Old Testament nor the Christian New. Eventually, he had put in his hands a little vest-pocket-sized New Testament that also included the books of Psalms and Proverbs. He read it all several times and made numerous marginal notes that documented the unfolding of his religious quest.

His mind was blown away by what he learned of the daily life and teachings of Jesus – his obvious caring for all kinds of human beings, his openness and acceptance toward the lowly, the marginalized, the outcast, and his forgiveness of those who would do him harm. These characteristics of the son of the Jewish carpenter from Galilee had a profound and permanent effect upon Jerry's attitudes and thinking. He could never be the same again.

All of this pondering Jerry laid out before me as we flew together across the Atlantic in Air Force Two after his escape (or release) from captivity – and in consequence of the generous determination of U.S. officials at the highest level to welcome him back in style. (I had flown over as a result of the State Department's acquiescence to Sis' request that I accompany her and the family on the flight it arranged to meet him in Germany.) During the extended conversations of our shared flight, I discovered what an extraordinary human being Jerry Levin really is – courageous, daring, perhaps even a bit foolhardy. Open and honest to a fault, unafraid to reveal his inner being, he quickly convinces you that he is just who he seems to be. No pretense. No false claims. No self-inflating piety.

His most awe-inspiring quality (perhaps achieved after some struggle) is his ability to transcend the fully human inclination to resent, to despise, to want revenge against those who kidnapped him and for almost a year held him against his will, deprived him of his family, his career, his freedom. He decided he couldn't, he wouldn't hang on to fears, anger, resentment, hatred. He saw nothing to be gained by focusing on a search for guilty persons to blame, no reason to expect they would ever be found and punished—and no benefit for him if they were.

Instead, he reasoned his way into accepting the fact that he had been an innocent bystander caught up in the swirling storms of the Middle-East conflict. He developed a mature understanding of the powerful forces of ethnic and religious tensions, accumulated grievances of the humiliated and fears of the traditionalist resisters of change. He was able to take into account the resentment of Arabs and Muslims against the perceived arrogance of the wealthy and powerful Christians and Jews of America and the West. Jerry did not excuse or justify in any way the criminal behavior of the extremists who attacked him, but he felt a compelling, spiritually guided impulse to forgive and get on with his life. That he has done with good spirit for more than 20 years.

His latest "mission" to stand as a silent witness to the call for peace between Palestinian Arabs and Israeli Jews, as a speaker of truth against cruelty and injustice, as an advocate for nonviolent resistance to violence is no peculiar quirk of a strange personality. It is a conscious, rational testimony to the belief of a spiritually advanced human being that love can overcome fear and that forgiveness and reconciliation can win out over hatred and violence—even in the heart of the conflicted West Bank.

Prologue

The reports in this book are adapted from the series of periodic news accounts, interviews, reflections and analyses I have been sending out via the internet on the effects of violence and nonviolence in the Middle East: specifically occupied Palestine, Israel, Jordan and Iraq. The essence of these essays which were titled "From The Inside Looking Out," are macro conclusions drawn from my micro experiences since early in 2002 when I became a full-time volunteer activist and communicator with the nonviolent Christian Peacemaker Teams (CPT), an international organization whose mission is to support violence-reduction efforts around the world.

Because of this work people who have some familiarity with my wife's and my story still ask two decades after my hostage ordeal why this one-time atheist and mainstream television-network journalist gave up a promising career to become a full-time volunteer member of CPT. I tell them it has everything to do with my kidnapping by the Hizballah in early March 1984 in Beirut, Lebanon where I had been running CNN's Middle East bureau. I was the first of what came to be known for awhile as the "forgotten American hostages." Until then I had believed quite emphatically and unquestioningly in what you might call the efficacy of violence. In other words, I was convinced that in certain situations violence worked. Coupled with that belief was also my agnostic disbelief in the entire concept of faith which perceived no rational connection between my "yes" belief in utilitarian logic justifying some kinds of violence and my always "no" disbelief in God.

But in captivity after ten days of intense contemplation, I reasoned and experienced a complete conceptual turnaround on both counts. Where nonviolence is concerned, I became convinced as to the inability of violence to achieve any condition that can be of permanent value to humankind and that the absence of nonviolence as a primary motivating force in terms of human behavior remains the most urgent problem the world needs to face up to without blinking if humankind is to survive.

But blinking, as we all know, is virtually uncontrollable especially when it comes to rationalizing violence and in particular the violence of retribution, revenge and preëmption. Like the little energy bunny, they keep on going. Nevertheless we need to face up to the awful effects of those prevalent forms of rationalized violence because, to begin with, too many people – especially here at home in the United States and, of course, elsewhere in both the coalitions of the willing and unwilling – only give lip service to relevant teachings about nonviolence as taught for example by Jesus during his Sermon on the Mount and centuries later by Mohandas Gandhi, Martin Luther King, Jr., Mubarak Awad and Nafez Assaily. It is clear, the lip servers by their actions are doing their best to turn Jesus into a nationalistic tribal god of war and render the others named irrelevant, impractical, downright foolish or – subversive.

Thoughts such as those in captivity led in time to my identifying the context of my captivity, which I describe as "the futility of violence." For instance, I don't see much difference between noncombatants killed as a result of the calloused, collateral damage of so-called Just War or those killed by the calloused, collateral damage of so-called Jihad. In both cases there is a reprehensible game of violence-rationalizing, violence-condoning going on, which is intentionally being pursued by too many Christians, too many Jews and too many Muslims – but happily not by all of any of the above. As a result, I am not concerned with just the futility of the violence of the so-called bad guys, but the futility of the violence of the so-called good guys, too. So the truth I discovered in captivity can be summed up by this: Violence doesn't work.

It turned out that during this period my wife Sis was coming to those same convictions. This 180-degree conceptual/behavioral turnaround took place soon after our ordeal began, so I had several months to ponder these new understandings and convictions.

On the 342nd day of my captivity – February 13, 1985 – I discovered one of the youths guarding me had been careless in securing the tight chain around my ankle that was meant to insure my continued captivity. I could be free of it. Shortly after midnight early in the morning of Valentine's Day I escaped. A day later I was accompanied protectively by the Syrian army out of Lebanon. That same night I was able to climb down from a small jet that CNN-founder Ted Turner had sent to Damascus to rush me to a reunion with Sis at a West German airport where we literally and joyfully fell into each others arms.

Suddenly in the midst of our wordless embrace she stopped and pointing to someone nearby whom I had never seen before said simply, "This is Landrum Bolling. He saved your life."

That's how I first met Landrum, an ageless Quaker Middle East specialist, former college president and chief executive of a major philanthropic foundation who also is author of the introduction to this book and editor of an earlier landmark work *Search For Peace in the Middle East* [Fawcett Publications, 1970]. At the time he was director of the Jerusalem Ecumenical Institute (also known as the Interfaith Peace Academy) located at Tantur on the border between Jerusalem and Bethlehem.

After that introduction I quickly learned (but not from him) that he was also the author of the nonviolent strategy that created the conditions for my "escape." The help took the form of an enlightened, step-by-step, person-to-person private diplomatic effort that had taken Sis and Landrum to Damascus where through his connections, on-scene introductions plus the logic of their presentations they succeeded in enlisting a humanitarian commitment by the Syrian government to do what it could to help.

Not long after, the "carelessness" of that youthful guard occurred and I was able to "escape." At the time I thought I had done it all by myself. In the face of what I have learned since, I am grateful for the efforts of all those who clearly made it happen – starting with Sis and Landrum. We are especially mindful that because of Landrum's enlightened, experienced and nonviolent counsel we do not bear the burden of the disgraceful violence-perpetuating Iran-Contra arms deal that scandalously scarred the return of many of those men kidnapped after me. [Sis dealt in detail with those episodes in her 1989 book about those uncertain months, *Beirut Diary*, and they were also reprised in a television docudrama aired in 1991, *Held Hostage*, where a remarkably faithful rendition of those events was reënacted by Marlo Thomas who was determined to do the story under the skillful guidance of producer Carol Polakoff who insisted that the inevitably necessary dramatic license be nevertheless faithful to the facts.]

After my release our lives moved in dramatically new directions – which before I was kidnapped would have been unthinkable. In keeping with our beliefs – and for almost 20 years now – she and I have stayed connected to and involved with the Middle East – in particular Palestine and Israel—in order to do and promote nonviolence. We have signed on, each in our own way, to the struggle against both physical walls and walls of the mind in Palestine and Israel because it's our belief that if the world can't get nonviolence "right" in the so-called Holy Land where the concept of community first began – and then almost immediately began to come unraveled – then the world won't be able to get it "right" anywhere else.

These days I am most often with CPT in Hebron in the West Bank, although both Sis and I took time out to be with the CPT team in Baghdad as the 2003 war was beginning in March and stayed on there into May. Sis is concentrating her efforts in Bethlehem where she has begun a program to teach teachers how to infuse the principles of nonviolence systemically and comprehensively in the schools where they work. We try to be together on the weekends.

Acknowledgments

Much has been given me by many in term of encouragement, constructive counsel and mentoring. At times that has meant proffering much-needed, tough-minded criticism (when it has come to curbing a vexing degree of incipient impulsiveness or potential over-the-top antipathy), whether I liked it or not. When I reflect on those names I realize that they mostly belong to people neither Sis nor I had met before our hostage experience and our subsequent turn to nonviolence activism, communication and teaching.

Soon after my return, Sis led me to Church of the Savior in Washington DC where I first met founders Gordon and Mary Cosby. After he heard me speak about the effects of the occupation on Palestine and Israel, Gordon said, "Jerry you sound like the prophets." I responded sincerely, "Gordon, I would not presume to place myself in such exalted company." Chuckling, Gordon responded, "Wait 'til you hear what they did to the prophets."

I had already met Landrum Bolling to whom Sis had been led by friends she met at the Church of the Savior's Potters House. His mentoring began on the Air Force Two flight back to the States after two days of medical examination at a military hospital in West Germany. I was scheduled to be on live CNN as soon as we touched down at Andrews Air Force Base, and en route he helped me formulate what I had been feeling about my ordeal. Here are the specific words I delivered that memorable February 18, 1985, which frankly, in my tired state, I hadn't been able to tease onto paper:

In the nearly one year of isolation and silence forced upon me, I was able to think and reflect (in a way I had never done before) on some of the deeper levels of my existence and life. Landrum Bolling described the experience to me as an "inward journey." It has deepened and given me a growing religious faith that no other experience in my life was able to motivate. If that was God's reason for putting me in solitary confinement, I thank him. And I thank him for my Jewish parents, my Christian wife and family and my Muslim friends. The prayers of my friends from all three faiths sustained me through a time I care not to repeat, but under the circumstances – looking back – I do not regret.

We have never ever been able to spend much time together since that first meeting because at 90+ Landrum still is always very much on the go working persistently at peacemaking in one overseas trouble spot or another.

In DC we quickly became members of World Peacemakers' founder Bill Price's *upstairs group* that met for years at Church of the Savior. I still haven't completed a manuscript with the working title *The Futility of Violence: Essays and Reflections on "Love Your Enemies"* that Bill has been pressing me to finish. To put that off I continue to pretend the draft he read which is in need of considerable editing and updating is not constantly within easy access in my whither-thou-goest laptop. Also in DC was Frank Wade, rector of St. Albans Episcopal Church, always cheerleading our efforts to make our way and find our roles in the struggle to promote and try to exemplify nonviolence.

Later in Birmingham the public affirmation and encouragement of Paul Zahl, dean of the cathedral, moved us profoundly to actively reconnect after a period of doubt as to whether we should keep at it. Equally important in that regard was our Birmingham neighbor Elizabeth Elliott, author of *Finding Palestine,* one of the courageous medical volunteers in Sabra and Chatilla refugee camps during the worst days of Israel's occupation in Beirut. Finally tired of waiting for me to do something about publishing my "From The Inside Looking Out" reports, she unasked sent some to Faith Sand. So here we are. Also in Birmingham our thanks to Catholic

Worker/Pax Christi friends and role models Shelley and Jim Douglass who have written and experienced more on the front lines of nonviolent activism than Sis or I ever will.

A similar encouraging influence has been John Stoner, instigator of the Every Church A Peace Church movement, whom we met only four years ago at a World Peacemakers retreat. He led us to CPT and since then during some very tough times has never been more than a cell phone or e-mail away with soothing and energizing words of encouragement plus other tangible forms of support and assistance.

Long before Sis and I became involved in nonviolence issues, especially in the Middle East, Darrel Meyers, founder of the Southern California Middle East Fellowship, and Don Wagner, the driving force behind the Palestinian Human Rights Campaign, the founder of Evangelicals For Middle East Understanding and currently director at North Park University's Center for Middle Eastern Studies, were devoting most of their energies to the issue. Don was one who, when I was missing, unasked called Sis one night out of the blue, without introduction, to offer assistance.

Sis received many such unsolicited calls during those long months. One night she got a call from a woman with a Middle Eastern accent, Dina, who said Don told her to call. It turned out Dina had been successful in her behind-the-scenes efforts to gain the release of her husband Salah Tamari, the highest ranking PLO leader to have been captured and imprisoned by the Israeli army during its Lebanon campaign. In an earlier incarnation Dina had been Jordan's late King Hussein's first wife.

In Palestine and Israel we have been befriended and spurred on by many whom we feel fortunate to have met, to have worked with and to have become friends, including Jerusalem-based Sabeel Palestine Liberation Theology Center's founder Naim Ateek, the Bethlehem Bible College's Awad brothers, Alec and Bishara plus Bishara's son Sami Awad, founder and compassionate leader of Holy Land Trust. In Hebron's Old City we continue to be awestruck by the persistent courage and determination of educator, social worker and translator Zleikha Muhtaseb who has been beaten severely several times by Israeli soldiers, border police and squatter-settlers while attempting to face down the occupation and creeping expropriations of Palestinian homes and shops. Also in Hebron and Jerusalem is my longtime mentor and factual resource, the gentle, creative Muslim exponent of nonviolent activism, Nafez Assaily who has endured an unwarranted share of severe injuries at the hands of armed Israelis.

In Jerusalem, Jeremy Milgrom is a constant inspiration. Also affirming and crucially supportive have been our colleagues in CPT who have had to put up at one time or another with my rudimentary cooking, complaints about the cold and habit of playing at odd hours my Sir Harry Lauder CD. I am also grateful to Faith Annette Sand for not only undertaking this publishing project, but also for also her patient ability to talk me out of my run-on, convoluted sentences, excruciating interjections, gee-whiz punctuation and shameful addiction to lazily coined words. In so doing she is making me out to be a much better writer than I really am. (See what I mean?)

Finally there is Sis ... always Sis.

1

Sometimes I Think Everything Is Area Z

Hebron, West Bank, Palestine, July 5, 2002

Beit Umar is a struggling Palestinian village – no more than a 15-minute drive during normal times from the center of Hebron where our CPT (Christian Peacemaker Team) is based, but times have not been normal in the West Bank (or Gaza) for decades, so this day it took a contingent of four CPTers about 45 minutes to get there.

First they squeezed into a Service car (like a jitney) which took them as far as an Israeli roadblock between Hebron and the town of Halhoul that borders Hebron on the north. After scrambling over the roadblock – a tightly packed mound of earth about six feet high completely blocking the road to vehicular traffic – they picked up another Service that took them to Beit Umar.

They were met by Jamal, who drove them over bumpy, deeply potholed and rutted roads to his home outside Beit Umar. The house is perched atop a ridge across a narrow valley from the Israeli settlement of Karmei Tsur. "I must spend about 250 shekels a month (about $50) just to keep my car running because of the bumps," Jamal sighed. What he keeps running is a banged-up relic that would have been junked long ago as untradable in the U.S.

From the edge of Jamal's home and his neighbors' on the ridge, Palestinian orchards and vineyards sweep down the hillside across the valley and up the other side to Karmei Tsur – up to Karmei Tsur on paper, that is. In reality, settlers have been steadily expanding the settlement's orchards and fields ringing Karmei Tsur over the years, using one excuse or another to encroach on more and more of Beit Umar's farmland – land that had been in Palestinian hands for centuries.

This time of year the theft of land often begins with the Palestinians suddenly being forbidden to tend to their fruit trees or grapevines. After a while, the settlers simply say the land is theirs – and that's that. Much legal wrangling in the courts inevitably ensues, often lasting many months or years and too often ends in either de jure or de facto defeat for the Palestinian farmers.

When the courts rule against the settlers, it's a de jure win for the Palestinians; but when the courts rule in favor of the Palestinians, either the army or the settlers often simply ignore the decision – making it a de facto defeat for Beit Umar's increasingly impoverished farmers. If you are a Palestinian you can't win for losing.

On the day of the CPT visit, settlers had been at it again, which is why – like so often before – CPT was asked in to see what it could do to remedy the situation. Jamal told CPT that first thing that morning settler security guards, always armed with menacing machine guns, had been shooing women harvesters off the latest piece of land on which they clearly had confiscating designs.

The problem for the Palestinians of Beit Umar is that their land is – in Oslo Accords terms – in Area C, which takes up more than 50 percent of the West Bank – a situation little understood by most in the United States. Area C has been retained by Israel for "security reasons" so, of course, it remains under complete and tight Israeli control. Despite their longstanding living off the land of Area C and despite their prior ownership, Palestinians with lands that are contiguous to the ever-expanding, land-greedy interloping Israeli settlements in Area C are always fair game – as far as the Israeli settlers are concerned–for expropriation of one kind or another.

Areas A and B were West Bank Palestinian lands, which in accordance with the Oslo agreements were turned over to the Palestinian Authority [area A] or mandated for partial control [area B]. During June 2002, however, the Sharon government turned back the clock and reoccupied all of areas A and B except Jericho. But even before that–Oslo notwithstanding–Israel had always been in effective control of more than 80 percent of the West Bank. Now it's 100 percent again.

"So, what is different for Palestinians in Area A [the largest municipalities], Area B [Palestinian villages], and Area C?" Jamal asked. Supplying the answer, he complained, "Nothing....Israel controls everything." Then with a sigh, he said, "Sometimes I think everything is just Area Z. There is no Palestine."

During the night there was sporadic gunfire from Karmei Tsur, which Jamal told us was usual. "Scares the children and makes sleep difficult," he said. In the morning, the CPT team headed off for the orchard, and met flustered women fruit pickers on their way back to Beit Umar because they had just been kicked out again by a settler security guard without having been able to get at a single plum or grape leaf.

When the CPT group arrived at the orchard, besides being told to go back by the security guard, they were also confronted by a protective Israeli army patrol. Although the security guard was adamant against giving in, the soldiers radioed their commander, who came by a few minutes later. No amount of jawboning could persuade him to let the women pick, although after almost an hour of wrangling he said CPT could. But in this case, the Palestinians on principle rejected the offer. They would have been willing to have the CPTers work alongside them, but, to them, the commander's solution was seen as harassment and fell far short of what they felt was their right.

So the CPTers headed back to Hebron. By this time the blockaded road situation had changed for the worse. They learned that all of Hebron had been put on a 24-hour curfew and the road they had taken from Halhoul to Beit Umar the day before was now blocked. A Service, however, was available to take them on a very round-about circuitous route from Beit Umar to Halhoul over dusty, jarring back roads. Getting from Beit Umar to Halhoul the day before would have taken about 20 minutes. Now it took 45. Because of the curfew, the CPTers were obliged to walk from the Halhoul roadblock to their base in the center of Hebron. That took an hour and 15 minutes.

2

Our God Will Kill Your God!

Hebron, West Bank, Palestine, July 10, 2002

My wife Sis and I thought it couldn't get any worse when we first started participating in and later shepherding fact-finding delegations to Palestine/Israel in the mid 1980s and early 1990s. But it has. When we began participating in a CPT delegation a year ago we could see for ourselves how wrong we had been. Nevertheless, even then we thought it couldn't get any worse. But it has.

For the first time in our experience Christian and Muslim children are begging in West Bank towns and cities. Rats are actually dying in the streets—possibly because there is no rat version of a land of milk and honey to which they can flee in order to survive.

"Happy are those who reject the advice of evil people, who do not follow the example of sinners or join those who have no use for God. Instead they find joy in obeying the law of the Lord." Those words, although they sound proverbial are actually taken from the very first psalm. They seem to signify that—at the time of their writing—the distinctive God of history had been leading the ancient Hebrews to the novel understanding that faith fully understood needs to be expressed—exemplified actually—in part through the sort of justice they were seeking for themselves and which they were sure they had been empowered from above to apply.

Events today in the Holy Land indicate quite dramatically that the theological clock has been turned back scandalously with what amounts to almost complete abandon. Radicals among the adversaries here (and supporters of both from outside their borders in the East and the West) are fostering the bombing of each other back, if not to the Stone Age, then to at least a time that predates the radical Mosaic attitudes towards retribution and revenge – when eye for eye, tooth for tooth represented a revolution in the concept of justice and violence.

This back-to-the-future regression, which makes an eye for an eye look like the good old days, extends all the way back to the time of Lamech – that boorish, churlish Hell's Angels, Sharks or Jets prototype who proudly boasted (see Gen 4:23) that "I have killed a young man because he struck me." [Read: "I have killed a Palestinian lad because he hit me with a stone...or an Israeli youngster because they were an easy target on whom to vent my rage."] "If seven lives are taken to pay for killing Cain," Lamech crowed, "77 will be taken if anyone kills [or tries to kill] me."

We truly live in a neo-Lamechian age – and have, perhaps, for at least a hundred years. The lack of global discipline, lack of selfless leadership, and no assurance of evenhanded accountability are having a disastrous effect in this tiny, terrified and terrifying strip of land. How else to explain the unregulated use of U.S.-built Apache helicopters capable of snuffing out multiple Palestinian lives with a single explosive burst or the posthumous lionizing of Palestinian young people who turn themselves into equally capable, culpable and deadly smart bombs or mini-F-16s?

Because of this frenzied disproportionate vengeance, a pre-Mosaic, Jesse James, O.K. Corral, recidivistic, rationalizing, barbaric vigilantism is being perpetrated pervasively on both sides of the Green Line. The authority of the message of Psalm 1, or Matthew 5:21-24 and 43-48 for that matter, is fading fast. The concept of a myopic, self-centered "never again" is being acted out by all the

People of the Book in accordance with the shocking sentiments expressed in one of the most celebrated psalms (137) that begins with words of epic and timeless pathos: "By the waters of Babylon we sat down, and there we wept...." However, it ends—putting it mildly—in startling and deplorable bathos: "Happy are those who pay you back for what you have done to us—who take your babes and smash them against the rock."

"Why do you look so angry?" one of our small group asked an Uzi-toting security guard. A grim settler had just led an Israeli army patrol up to our little group of CPT and Quaker fact-finders that had been waiting expectantly and hopefully in a field outside the Palestinian village of At-Tuwani—in the hills southeast of Hebron—for someone in authority to answer our call for help. We had gotten in touch with local police on a cell phone a half hour before to ask help for the villagers who were helpless to deal with mooning Israeli kids from the nearby settlement of Ma'on. Before that the brats had been bathing brazenly and nakedly in what had been an Palestinian well but which lately had been confiscated and put under settler lock and key.

The police said they would send the army. When the troopers arrived, escorted by that scowling Ma'on security guard, it was clear they were there on Ma'on's behalf, not At-Tuwani's.

Our complaint had no constructive effect on the security guard, which was no surprise, nor on the commander of the soldiers, also no surprise, although we had hoped he might try to rein in the security guard a bit. Instead he clearly was concerned with making as few waves as possible—for the settlers not the villagers.

The security guard went so far as to tell us that we CPT and Quaker visitors had no right to be where we were because the land we were in was Area C—the notorious military security zone that constitutes more than half the West Bank and where the Israel military is a law unto itself. From now on, the security guard yelled, we had to get permission from authorities in Ma'on to visit the area. The army commander did not contradict.

That's when the security guard was asked, "Why do you look so angry?"

"I was born angry!!!" he literally snarled.

A few days earlier in the Old City of Hebron, a 30ish settler, clutching the hand of a four-year-old boy, probably his son, seeing me intently observing two Israeli army troopers detaining a couple of Palestinian youths, started spitting in my direction. [Spit-spit] "Our God will kill your God," he shrieked. Then [spit-spit], pointing to my red CPT cap and red CPT armband he yelled, "You have a bloody head. Get out of here. We will kill you." Then he led the little boy into the yeshiva in front of which they had been standing—presumably for the lad's latest lesson in scripture.

And so the fanatic, uncompromising, debilitating beat (beating?) goes on: a physically, emotionally, and spiritually draining demented dance of death—the theme music of the Four Horsemen, who win every time peacemakers lose.

Has the promise gone from "The Promised Land?" Right now it surely appears on the verge of going. Just as "Holy Land" these days is a contradiction in terms, so has Palestine become "The Broken-Promise Land."

3

The Settlers Are Angry

Hebron, West Bank, Palestine, July 12, 2002

For the past several weeks I have been overwhelmed by a mournful feeling of conceptual déjà vu. Recent events are confirming that certain semantic chickens, which I have been pondering for quite some time, have come home to roost. Here's why.

Last September the *Birmingham News* (my hometown newspaper) ran a commentary I had written after getting back from a late August trip to Palestine and Israel. The *News* quite accurately headlined the piece "Israel Inflicting Pogroms on Palestinians".

I proposed that notion because it seemed to me – and still does – that when Palestinians describe their very real and terrible, unceasing calamity as a holocaust, they are taking a stand on the wrong semantic hill. Insisting on that kind of equivalency leaves them and supporters open to claims of insensitive hyperbole – and thus inevitably sparks an unseemly squabble over statistics, i.e., how many state of Israel-sponsored ethnic murders of noncombatant Palestinians and other human rights abuses does it take to make a second holocaust?

That's not the best argument to be expending one's energy on when the reality of the Palestinian plight is such that no exaggeration (or at least what could be termed thus) is necessary. So why belabor the holocaust point, I argued, when pogrom is a perfectly functional and terrifyingly precise, accurate label for what is happening in the occupied territories?

Today militant, acquisitive Israelis, many of whom are confident they are appropriately emulating Joshua, are in fact acting out a topsy-turvy replay of the persecutions dramatized in the famous Broadway musical drama of the 1960s, "Fiddler on the Roof." [Ed: "Fiddler" celebrated Jewish fortitude and an irrepressible spirit in the face of the vicious, destructive and often deadly pogroms that took place in Eastern Europe and Czarist Russia as the 19th century was winding down. In fact it was the sadistic pogroms in the East and the notorious anti-Semitic Dreyfus affair in France that so frightened and obsessed the sophisticated and culturally assimilated Viennese journalist Theodor Herzl that in time he was moved to conceive modern Zionism, the latter day Exodus for contemporary Jews in need of a safe haven, a new place to call home that would be uniquely theirs. Unfortunately for the Arabs already living in Palestine (the future Palestinians), the spot finally designated, was already home to more than 700,000 of them.]

Ironically in this real-life, updated revival of "Fiddler on the Roof," Palestinians have become protagonists – Tevye and his family – while their Israeli adversaries have become frightening replicas of 19th-century Cossacks; and the villages and towns of the West Bank and Gaza have become Anatekva, Tevye's small oppressed village, located beyond the pale.

Israelis can no longer claim exclusive rights to the term "pogrom" because it no longer applies solely to the terrible practices that made their forbearers so desperate to flee Eastern Europe and Russia as the 19th century was winding down. Now 21st-century pogroms, as exemplified by the dreary and deadly practice of Israeli-army-inflicted, collective punishments of Palestinians coupled with the confiscatory rampages of settlers, are as destructive, debilitating, demeaning, humiliating and horribly violent as were the ones inflicted 100 and more years ago on Jews in Poland, Lithuania, Russia and elsewhere. As a result, "pogrom" historically and culturally has become a bitterly ironic noun which, when applied to the current situation, cannot be easily snarled away by critics.

Naturally a number of mailed and e-mailed reactions to my thoughts about pogroms were neither complementary nor friendly.

10

But events all along and especially during the past two weeks in Gaza as well as in and around Hebron have aroused confirmation of this view from Israelis not on the left but in the center and even on the near-right as well. What has sparked this admission in part has been settler actions and reactions in Hebron (where CPT is based) that followed the Sharon-administration-approved liquidation of a Hamas violence-fomenting militant via a made-in-America F-16 and its one-ton-explosive payload. Also killed in the massive blast were members of his family, as well as several clearly innocent nearby children and adults.

Once the smoke of that attack cleared away, it was inevitable that two tragically uncreative, chaos-escalating, violent shoes would be dropped: the first, murderous retaliation by some militant Palestinian faction or another, and the second by Hebron Old City settlers who have a history of taking advantage of the inevitable Israeli army clamp-downs on Palestinians in the name of security in order to enable the relentless extension by stealth of their limited, but expanding, domain.

Even before the tragically predictable, retributive Palestinian ambush of settlers on the outskirts of Hebron, settlers in the Old City began to take advantage of the heightened security measures instituted by the Israeli army in the wake of the Gaza liquidation mission. The first incident under cover of curfew took place late at night. Settlers broke through the back wall of a string of Palestinian shops bordering the yeshiva in the Old City settlement of Beit Romano where they moved in, trashed, looted, changed the locks at the front of the shops and refused to leave until Palestinian protests finally motivated the Israeli soldiers to persuade – very gingerly – the invaders to leave. The entire incursion had to have taken place with the complete knowledge of the Israeli army because at least two of its outposts are within spitting distance of the scene of the crimes.

Once the settlers left, that, of course, should have been that; but where settler and Israeli army occupation practices are concerned, it rarely is. True to frustrating, obfuscating, bureaucratic form, it was not this time either. When the Palestinian owners of the shops sought permission from the military to cut away the offending locks so that they could regain possession of their stores and add up their losses, they were put off by army officials who kept promising that permission would come "tomorrow in the morning...." So far that hasn't happened. [Ed: And the stores have remained permanently closed, ever since.]

At the end of the week – using the funeral of those killed in the ambush – the already furious settlers, who had been stirred up Marc Antony style by young toughs at the service, set off on a destructive rampage through the Palestinian old market section of the Old City. Israeli police and Israeli soldiers stood by passively. When asked why, one officer said simply, "The settlers are angry. When they are like that, we don't control them." When the military finally got the settlers to leave, one bystander, a 14-year-old Palestinian girl had been shot to death, her younger brother wounded, others injured, windows shot out and some property trashed.

After a lull, settlers shielded by several soldiers successfully invaded a Palestinian home bordering the Old City settlement of Avraham Avinu. The home, known as the Sharabati House, had been a kind of museum and library – an important unofficial repository of ancient Arab manuscripts dating back, we have been told, to the time of Saladin, as well as artifacts, aged objects and equally old documents, all of which comprised an important element of the collective Hebron Old City Palestinian community's memory.

The settlers ransacked and trashed most of the house and burnt the library. A week later acrid smoke still hangs heavy in the rooms of the shattered home and exhibition space. Other evidence of the thoroughness of the settlers' destruction is still evident throughout most of the rooms. It will take days to straighten out the mess. [Ed: A year later the family, worn down by the settlers' destructive and menacing harassment and the Israeli army's indifference, moved out of the Old City for good.]

The latest incidents up to the writing of this report took place in the street below the CPT apartment, located at the edge of the poultry market section of the Old City. A throng of settler women, preceded by stone and rock throwing settler kids, broke into the area twice last Tuesday morning menacing Palestinian shopkeepers and bystanders and breaking several dozen eggs in the store of one of our neighbors. Then they ran off screeching and yelling as they penetrated more deeply into the market. Israeli police who were slow to respond to CPT's calls for help stood by passively, seemingly content to let whatever was to be – be.

The military was even slower to react. But once soldiers did show up, they entered the area, taking off slowly after the women. When they caught up with them, they gently escorted them out of the market, but made no arrests. [Included next is a copy of the CPT news release giving a more detailed account of the incidents in the poultry market which includes an account of the bruising attack on our CPT colleague LeAnne Clausen.]

A high-ranking advisor to the Sharon government on "settlement security" has been quoted in the Israeli press as saying the settler rampage following the funeral was "a pogrom against the Palestinians of Hebron with no provocation on the Palestinian side." Their actions preceding and following that deadly event – described above – clearly were more of the same.

We can hope that in time such candor and such truths concerning the still-evolving neo-pogrom era, when expressed by more Israelis in the center, will abet a process that can help finally to set the Palestinians free from oppression. That in turn could free Israelis from the threat of indiscriminate violent reprisals, which too often are killing their own children and adults.

But we cannot expect that to happen any time soon. Why? Because the pogroms in the form of settler vigilantism and Israeli army collective punishments, when paired with Palestinian attacks, proactive or reactive on Israeli noncombatants, are the wounds most in need of healing these days, the sickness most in need of a cure. And that is just not happening.

For Immediate Release

CPTers Attacked by Rampaging Settler Women

by Jerry Levin

HEBRON WEST BANK – Several young Israeli settler women and youths invaded Hebron's Old Market area twice Tuesday, July 30, 2002 assaulting Palestinian shopkeepers and members of the Christian Peacemaker Team (CPT) who were trying to intervene and document the incident.

The first disturbance began at about 9:15 in the morning in the street below the CPT apartment. Four settler boys started throwing stones and rocks over the barricade separating the Palestinian market from Shuhada Street. CPTers phoned the police and alerted soldiers stationed on a roof across the street to the attack.

As CPTers Jerry Levin, LeAnne Clausen and Janet Shoemaker reached the street to investigate, two young settler women came through the barricade and began throwing stones at an elderly Palestinian man nearby. Clausen left the doorway to protect the man from the settlers.

A settler woman demanded Levin's camera and tried to grab it. Levin, who was blocking entry to the building, passed the camera to Shoemaker who was standing inside behind him.

When the settler women noticed Clausen photographing them trying to get past Levin, one moved towards her, trying to grab the camera. Clausen, trying to shield the camera with her body, was knocked down by one of the women who then bent her fingers back and struck her repeatedly with her fists. Meanwhile, a second woman hit her with stones and a third began kicking her in the back of the head. Levin, trying to block the settlers' blows, got down and covered Clausen with his body to protect her and the camera.

Three Israeli soldiers came through the barricade. The settler boys stopped throwing stones, but a woman standing no more than three feet away from Clausen threw a chunk of asphalt in her face.

The women then began moving further into the market. A few minutes later a patrol of about ten Israeli soldiers entered the market through the barricade and gently escorted the women out of the area.

At 12:45 PM young settler women again charged through the barricade and attacked the poultry store next to the CPT apartment, taunting and hitting the owner, his sons and breaking several dozen eggs. Still screaming they stormed further into the market area.

Calls for help from CPT brought an Israeli police van. Once again police stood watching from the safety of Shuhada Street. After several minutes, a contingent of some ten soldiers arrived, headed into the market and a few minutes later escorted the settler women out. The soldiers made no attempt to restrain or arrest any of them.

Palestinian shopkeepers expressed their anger to CPTers about the indifference of the police and the soldiers' solicitous treatment of the settler women. One angry elderly Palestinian man yelled at the soldiers. "Our God is watching this. And he will not let this happen." An Israeli soldier hearing him stopped, turned and said very slowly, "He is our God. And he has saved us."

4

Looking for the Big Fish

Hebron, West Bank, Palestine, August 8, 2002

Ever since the reoccupation last month of H1, the Israeli army has been reimposing curfew every night at seven or eight. H1 is the portion of Hebron which had been given over to the Palestinian Authority to rule as a result of the late 1990s, post-Oslo, Wye River Accords.

The curfews have served the obvious, time-immemorial purpose of theoretically keeping an occupying force out of harm's way by penning up the occupied in their houses. Curfews, however, in Hebron and elsewhere, are not leak proof. As a result, as dusk ends and curfew begins, a nightly ritual takes place – the rounding up of the Shebab.

The Shebab are, strictly speaking, Palestinian teenage boys and unmarried young men, but the term is more loosely applied to any Palestinian male under 30. This is the age group, current history has demonstrated, which is or potentially is – with respect to the Israeli army and settlers – the most lethal and, therefore, the most notorious. It is the one, which for a variety of other reasons too – including energy, strength, agility, occupation and simply sheer youth – is most often likely to be in the streets after curfew begins.

For instance, young men and older boys may be slow in closing down the sales space where they work in Hebron's main market place – Bab iZaweyya – simply because they hope to squeeze out a few more shekels in sales before shutting down for the night as ordered.

Another group, like those in the market, is made up of young men willing to risk being in the streets as curfew begins – the ubiquitous taxi and Service drivers trying to eke out a last round of fares before packing it in. Then there are Palestinians still out in their personal cars trying to take care of last-minute errands.

Right around the corner, however, from this waning activity and about 25 yards down a side street from Bab iZaweyya is an Israeli army checkpoint at an intersection the army calls Tarpot Junction and which CPT and the Palestinians call the Dubboya Street checkpoint. It straddles the dividing line between H1 and H2, the section of the Old City completely and perpetually under Israeli army control because of the four tiny Jewish settlements of Beit Hadassah, Beit Romano, Avraham Avinu and Tel Rumeida, established there in the decades following the 1967 war.

As curfew begins, the two-man Israeli army patrol staffing the checkpoint heads into Bab iZaweyya on a mission to round up young male stragglers driving into or through the now-emptied market or those who are tardily headed home on foot. As vehicles pull into the area or as a young man walks through, they are ordered to stop. The roundup usually takes some 20 minutes – or until what seems to be the nightly goal of bagging about 14 or 16 young men.

All – including the drivers – are herded against a nearby wall and their IDs lifted. Once the roundup is completed, they are marched to the checkpoint where again they are lined up against a wall across a small open space from the DCO's (the military's district coördinating officer) shack. It's a tiny jerry-built guardhouse with a desk where the officer in charge can report information he finds on the commandeered IDs to an Israeli intelligence center for checking.

Because of the potential for confrontation, Bab iZaweyya is the place where an intentional CPT early evening amble is likely to begin. The patrolling CPTers, if they haven't been diverted to some incident more pressing, will follow the detainees as they are being herded to the checkpoint. The aim and hope is that the CPT presence will speed up the ID-checking process and motivate the soldiers to let the men have water and be allowed to squat or sit on the ground, if they wish, while they wait for the results of the ID check.

Each Israeli army patrol seems to have a specific personality. Some soldiers, at least in the presence of CPTers, will recognize the detainees' humanity by treating them with respect. Others will not—and often this depends on the attitude of the officer in charge. In his presence they tend to reflect his stance. Out of sight, they may not.

We have encountered—so far—two categories of DCO personalities: an almost "good cop/bad cop" dichotomy. A captain who tells us his name is Marwan, which we doubt because that is a typically Palestinian name not Israeli, is cold and surly to CPT. He doesn't like talking to us and so simply refuses to discuss what's happening because, he angrily explains, CPT has no right to be standing in his checkpoint and questioning him about the detainees. "You CPTers should not be here. Israel does not recognize you. Go. Leave."

After getting those assertions off his chest, he storms back into the shack. But we don't leave. Instead we slip into the shadows where Captain "Marwan" is not likely to see us when he comes back out. We are abetted by one of the noncoms who actually suggests we wait out of sight, apparently not minding our continual observation so long as it does not look as if he and his partner are allowing this.

In fairness to Captain "Marwan," it does not take any longer (about an hour) to check the IDs of the detainees when he is in charge than when another officer, a lieutenant who calls himself "Golan," is there doing the checking. (We also have our doubts as to the validity of his name since other soldiers there have confided to us that it is not.)

However, unlike Marwan, Golan talks with us and doesn't have to be asked to let the men squat or sit down. His soldiers (often the same ones there when Marwan is in charge) even initiate giving the detainees water. Golan doesn't mind explaining to us why there is the inevitable roundup of Shebab at the beginning of curfew. "I am looking for the big fish," he says with a self-satisfied grin. "This is how we catch them. I like to catch the big fish."

"Who are big fish?"

"I tell you," he says proudly. "In the spring, right here, just like now, I catch a big fish. You remember the terrorist killing of...? (He names the incident.) Well, we know what terrorists look like. So one night just like this we catch the man who did it. Can you imagine it? This terrorist-looking guy was just walking around like those guys here. We check his ID and we catch him – the big fish. Maybe we catch another big fish tonight."

"But tonight it was already getting dark when your soldiers stopped the cars. How could they see the faces inside well enough to know whether or not they were terrorist-looking men?"

"Never mind. We know."

"But if they look like terrorists, how come you let most of them go, after you have their IDs checked?"

"Never mind. That's how we catch them. And, I tell you, we catch them. The computer tells us if they are wanted. Then we arrest them. But we are not terrorists. So, if they are not wanted, we let them go."

A few minutes later, all the detainees are released except one. Golan with a gleeful look on his face bounces out of the shack to tell us, "You see, this one is a big fish."

"How do you really know?"

"The computer says he is wanted."

"Does it say he is a big fish?"

"Well, maybe not so big this time. We'll see. We are still checking."

A few minutes later the last of the evening's detainees is re-leased. "He is lucky," Golan says. "He was not a big fish tonight. Just a little gold fish. But maybe some night we will catch him again. And he might not be so little."

Meanwhile, the Palestinian almost-big-fish heads back toward Bab iZaweyya and the car he was forced out of an hour and a half earlier. In it he finds his thoroughly frightened eleven-year old son sitting in the dark – too immobilized by fear to do anything but wait uncertainly, although hopefully, for his father's safe return.

5

Have a Nice Day

Hebron, West Bank, Palestine, August 24, 2002

Almost every Sunday I make the six- to seven-hour trek from Hebron to the Palestinian village of Ibillin in Northern Galilee, near Haifa, so that I can spend a quick 24-hour holiday with Sis. Each time I cross the Green Line dividing Palestine from Israel I am reminded of Dorothy remarking to Toto with wide-eyed wonder that they weren't in Kansas anymore.

One of the many differentiating features between life in the Kansas of the West Bank and the Oz of Israel, is a small one. Nevertheless it is one that I find difficult to put out of my mind. It's this: Workers in the Israeli service and retail industries invariably end conversations, inquiries, sales, what-have-you not with "goodbye," but with a cheery "Have a nice day." No matter what one does or where one goes in Israel, one will not be immune to the incessant salutation, "Have a nice day."

For me the semantic phenomenon often starts at the Central Bus Station in West Jerusalem where I catch a bus to Haifa. I ask the woman in the information booth what time the next one will leave. She tells me. I say, "Thank you." She says, "Have a nice day." Then, if I have time, I walk over to the coffee shop and buy a cappuccino and a sweet roll. When I pay, the counterperson instead of saying "Thank you," delivers the currently preferred alternative, "Have a nice day."

Last week, I bought a new memory card for my digital camera at an Office Depot in Haifa. (Remember that memory card, because I'll have more to say about its predecessor later.) After I paid the clerk, she said, "Have a nice day." Earlier we rented a car in Jerusalem to do some sightseeing. As I collected the keys, the Hertz clerk launched us with a genial "Have a nice day." Later we stopped for gas where a solicitous attendant after filling our tank and washing our windshield saw us off with an energetic wave and a boisterous "Have a nice day."

Meanwhile, in the West Bank one encounters a grimmer version of the pervasive pleasantry. For instance, Sis and I were taking a visiting friend to see Bethlehem, but first we had to pass through the heavily guarded barricaded checkpoint which separates Jerusalem from Bethlehem. In line behind us was a Muslim woman who told us she hoped that she would not have any problem getting through because she had a noontime appointment—just 45 minutes off—at the only hospital in the West Bank with the medication needed to ease the condition of her cancer-stricken sister. She had to get there by noon, or the doctor she needed to issue a prescription would be gone for the rest of the day.

After a quick glance at our passports, Sis and I and our friend were waved on by the Israeli soldier checking identification papers. But when we looked back to see how the woman was doing, we saw the soldier shove her identification card back at her and then wave her off. We could see her pleading with him to let her pass. But he wouldn't. So, we went back to try to change his mind.

Clearly annoyed by our sudden interference, he explained testily, "She does not live in Bethlehem." The woman showed him and us other papers prepared by a Jerusalem doctor attesting to 1) the need for the medicine, 2) that the hospital in Bethlehem was the only place to get it, and 3) that the woman needed to meet the doctor, who would write the prescription, by noon.

But still the soldier would not change his mind. "Her papers," he told us impatiently, "are no good."

"Do you think she is a bomber?"

"No, but her papers are no good."

"Then why don't you check them? You heard her say that she has an appointment in half an hour."

"That is not my problem."

Another soldier came over and tried to shoo us away. But we weren't in a mood to be shooed. Finally the first one took the woman's ID and called some information into a portable phone.

Surprise! Surprise! Seconds later—not minutes—he said ruefully, "She may go."

As we and the woman walked happily by him, the clearly miffed soldier said sarcastically, "Have a nice day."

A few days later as I started to walk across a major Israeli highway south of Bethlehem, a Palestinian man driving a small truck—without looking carefully—suddenly made a U-turn, cutting off an army Jeep headed in the same direction. It missed hitting the truck by a few inches. Standing 30 yards away—astonished by the near miss—I watched four soldiers pile out of the Jeep and without a word swiftly rush the car, pull the driver out through the window and start beating him. So I began taking pictures with my digital camera.

Israeli soldiers do not, under most circumstances, want their pictures taken. There are countless stories of them breaking offending cameras, so I knew I was taking a risk by photographing four of them beating a Palestinian. And I was right. Suddenly one of them glanced up and saw me clicking away. He shouted something to his buddies. All four stopped kicking and punching the Palestinian and quickly moved on me yelling "No pictures! No pictures!" as they advanced.

I knew my camera was in for it (and maybe me too) unless I could think of something effective to say or do. Remembering the old football strategy—the best defense is an offense—I yelled at the soldiers as they were striding angrily up to me, "I am an American and we don't do in America what you are doing to that man." Of course, I was counting on the fact that they wouldn't have heard of Rodney King. That specific worry, however, was moot, because one of them simply grabbed my camera without a word, pulled out the memory card and with a sneer crushed it in his large calloused palm.

"Are you going to buy me a new one," I snapped.

Shrugging off my scathing remonstrance, he simply snarled, "Go! Go!"

Meanwhile, as this was happening, all four soldiers were standing with their backs to the Palestinian man. Taking advantage of their shifted focus, he quickly slipped back into his car and drove off in the opposite direction.

Once the car was far enough down the road, I said to the soldier who had ruined my memory card, "Okay, I'll go," and again weakly added, "But one of you guys needs to buy me a new memory card."

All the soldiers simply laughed and began walking away. Then one of them, as if struck by a gleeful afterthought, turned back to me and said with a facetious grin, "Have a nice day."

6

School Daze in Hebron
Part 1

Hebron, West Bank, Palestine, November 8, 2002

I wouldn't have left Hebron the last day in August except for the inconvenient fact that Sis' and my visas were on the verge of expiring. My reluctance to leave was due to the day following being the start of school in Hebron. The new school year would undoubtedly mean the inevitable resumption of almost daily fright and exasperation for too many students, faculty and school administrators.

Too true.

Each e-mailed weekly update or more urgent news alert from CPT Hebron, which we downloaded each day during our speaking tour in the Middle West and East Coast, was a persistent reminder that our misgivings were more than justified. It was not pleasant to read about the dreary story being told anew about the frequent disruptions of classes by soldiers barging into playgrounds and classrooms, the terrorizing of students and adults inside and outside the schools with tear gas and percussion grenades and even more lethal weapons, as well as the constant capricious shut-downs by Israeli soldiers and border police. All the foregoing, the reports confirmed, were once again the infuriating rule rather than the exception. And I wasn't there to help.

So it was with great relief my first morning back in the Old City that I joined colleagues on their early morning patrol of schools in CPT's monitoring area near the historic Ibrahimi Mosque (and synagogue). Four of the schools are lined up almost side by side along a single block 50 yards down a sloping street from a major checkpoint which separates Israel's tightly guarded Mosque Special Security Zone from the rest of Hebron.

As we made the half-mile walk from the CPT apartment to the schools, my partner Kristin Anderson told me that an expectation for the week was an increase in military harassment, because the upcoming Friday night and Saturday Jewish Sabbath would mark an important event on the settler calendar: the reading of the section of the Torah detailing the story of Abraham's coming to Hebron. An influx of ecstatic religious and secular ultranationalist Orthodox Jews was expected – several thousand perhaps – to celebrate the event. In anticipation, the Israeli army the day before had slapped a curfew back on the area that had been enjoying a couple of week's relief from that debilitating indignity.

Because religious occasions with nationalist overtones have in the past inspired settler rampages in the Old City, the days preceding have always meant not only heightened military alert but also an inevitable testy edginess by the sizable army and border police contingents charged with maintaining order in H2 (the sector of the city awarded to Israel by the Wye River Accords).

Fewer than 500 settler residents – guarded by 2,000 soldiers and border police – live in H2. They have relentlessly been increasing the size of their tiny enclave for more than two decades, stealthily, illegally and only reluctantly sharing it – to put it mildly – with the 45,000 Palestinians still hanging on there. So when we showed up in front of the Hebron Boys Basic School gate, we were not surprised to find that the two soldiers usually staffing the checkpoint had sallied down the hill and were quietly telling the headmaster to shut down. No reason was given – just shut down.

However, as students kept arriving at the gate and even though the soldiers' presence was potentially intimidating, they made no move physically to stop the kids from going in. It appeared that maybe CPT's presence might help the headmaster successfully get the two relatively diffident soldiers to relent. But shortly before the 8:00 AM bell rang, after being defied for about a half hour, one made a call on his portable phone and as the bell began clanging, an army Jeep – as if on cue – rolled up. An officer leaned out the window and tersely told the headmaster that he had ten minutes to clear the school.

As the angry and frustrated headmaster told his teachers to send the students home, he complained, "This is 15th time since school starts that the soldiers do this! How can we teach? How can students learn?" (A few days later, after checking his attendance book, he scrupulously told me that actually his school had been shut down only 14 times since the start of school.)

The next day, as school was ending, CPT received a frantic call from the headmistress of the only girls' school on the block. "Please come," she said. "Soldiers come into school and take one of our girls." As colleague Christine Caton and I hurried down the hill from the checkpoint to the school we came across a boy, maybe six or seven years old, crying in the street and through his tears asking for help. We guessed that he was the girl's brother and when we met the headmistress inside the school, it turned out we were right.

The girl, the headmistress told us, a 14-year-old, was being detained by the soldiers at the checkpoint. When we had passed through it on the way down the hill to the school, we had seen no one being held there, so we guessed that when the soldiers saw us coming, they hid her. Sure enough, as we walked back to the checkpoint – with the tearful boy following about 25 yards behind – we saw the soldiers grab a girl they clearly had been detaining and push her into an empty room in a building alongside the checkpoint. The little boy pointed to the girl and himself and then stopped – as if waiting for something good to happen.

When we asked the soldiers why they had come into the school, ordered the girl out of class and then tried to hide her from us, they told us it was none of our business. Then they led her – defiantly it seemed – out of their hideaway room and over to the other side of the street where one of the soldiers ordered her to stand facing the wall. When we walked over and started talking to her, we were told to go away. We said that *not* going away is our job. The soldier snapped back, "You will not talk to her and you will stay over there," pointing to a spot about 50 feet up the street from the girl.

Then it became a waiting game, perhaps simply to frustrate our attempt to free the girl and show us who was boss. In the interim I started taking pictures. The expected happened. One of the soldiers yelled, "No pictures. No pictures." I shuttered the camera, not wanting to take the chance of having my memory card confiscated and crushed as had happened before. But that reminded me of a potential option with respect to visual documentation, which I hoped might help free the girl. "I'll call TIPH on my cell phone," I told Christine, which I did noisily so that the soldiers could hear my summons.

TIPH (Temporary International Presence Hebron) is a much larger (and officially recognized by all sides) observation presence in Hebron. A creation of the Oslo Accords, its 42-person operational staff is recruited from several partnering European nations and Turkey. TIPH observers patrol the city, usually in twos, documenting and filing reports on potential or actual violent incidents plus events that are simply humiliating or inconveniencing. TIPH reports are not made public, but they are filed with the governments of the organizing coalition, as well as with Israel and the Palestinian National Authority.

With respect to picture taking, when the agreement forming TIPH was hammered out, both still and motion picture photography was specifically permitted. Nevertheless, Israeli soldiers don't like their too often scandalous and over-the-top bullying, belittling and often violent behavior caught live on TIPH's very candid cameras, so those involved often will try to bluff the observers into stopping their picture taking by telling them that the army has the right to order them to shut down.

The observers, of course, know better. So they keep right on shooting, even while the soldiers (who know better than to physically attempt to prevent them) are screaming angrily at them to stop. I've seen many a normally soft-spoken and always polite TIPH observer go at it jaw-to-jaw with soldiers or officers—much like umpires digging in their heels at the in-your-face attempts at intimidation by baseball players—and never have seen one back down yet. What usually happens is that the soldiers, knowing perfectly well what the truth about picture taking is, finally back down.

Just the fact that the incident is being caught on tape can sometimes cause the bullying (or whatever) to wind down and stop. That is what happened in the case of the girl we were trying to help. The next day, as I was on patrol in front of her school, she shyly walked up to me and said softly, "Thank you."

But those two incidents were minor compared to what took place two days later on the Jewish Sabbath marking Abraham's coming to Hebron.

(TO BE CONTINUED)

7

School Daze in Hebron
Part 2

Hebron, West Bank, Palestine, November 14, 2002

By the middle of the week leading up to the big annual Fall Friday night and all-day Saturday settler Sabbath celebration in Hebron, featuring the reading of Genesis 23 (the portion of the Torah which tells the story of Abraham obtaining a piece of land there from a certain Hittite inhabitant) the army and the border police appeared to be tensing up, as well as gearing up, for trouble.

An influx of 10,000 religious and secular ultranationalist Orthodox Jews and fellow travelers from not only Israel but elsewhere was being predicted by their sources. So, from about Wednesday on, Israeli military and police forces began to restrict Palestinian activity, imposing lengthening curfews and launching more frequent guns-at-the-ready patrols into the Old City. That's how Palestinians are protected by the military authorities from settler harassment and attacks. Palestinians are ordered into their homes and told to stay there.

On Friday, November 2nd, because it was a Muslim holy day, there was, of course, no school. Nevertheless curfew was imposed early and not lifted. We wondered what the situation would be like at the schools on Saturday morning when they would reopen

and the number of settlers and their supporters who would supposedly be flocking into the area was likely to be the most concentrated. At 7:15 AM when CPTers Kristin Anderson, Mary Yoder
and I–plus three members of a visiting Quaker fact-finding delegation–approached the four schools we have been most concerned
about this school year, we found out in a hurry.

As we walked down the hill from the checkpoint, we could
see hundreds of boys and girls in the street bordering the schools
milling about in swirling eddies of excited, yet hesitant, youthful
humanity. A knot of worried and clearly furious male teachers was
congregated helplessly in front of one of the schools. By now the
gates to all three boys' schools should have been wide open with
kids streaming into schoolyards from every direction, but all three
were shut and no one was getting into the two on either side of
Marief School for Boys. But at that one, even though no one was
being let in, neither did it look as if those already in the school-
yard were trying to get out. From a distance we could see the
frazzled headmaster and some of his equally frustrated staff trying
to shoo students huddling inside the gate out into the street, but
the apprehensive kids weren't budging.

In the meantime that cacophonous crush of youngsters outside
the gates was swelling ever more loudly as arriving school-bound
youngsters streamed noisily into the area from adjoining streets.
Suddenly a couple of border police Jeeps, their top lights flashing,
roared unswerving from around a corner right down the center of
the street, scattering all of us in every direction like scampering
rabbits or startled chickens.

When we finally made it to the Marief Boys School gate, we
found not only the sputtering headmaster but also the equally
distressed headmaster of Hebron Basic Boys School. He told us
that at about 6:45, as his kids were beginning to show up at his
gate, border police arrived also and told him that curfew was on
and that he should not unlock the gate. He was ordered instead to
start sending all children home.

But easier said than done.

The furious headmaster told us that a few minutes later other police in more Jeeps invaded the area, shooting off a couple of rounds of tear gas right into the throng of now venue-less students. Not being sure where the next attack would come from, the kids were literally thrashing about uncertainly after each salvo – trapped in the roadway by doubt as to how to get away – much like sailboats caught in "irons."

These provocative acts, we CPTers could see – now that we were in the thick of the still-evolving episode – were exacerbating the children's fear and uncertainty as to just what they could do, as opposed to what the Israelis were saying they should do – a typical Catch-22 for the young Palestinians and their hapless teachers. The menacing Jeeps stirring up dust as they sped by, their loud speakers blaring terse orders to everyone to go home and stay there, only served to keep pupils still stuck in the Marief school-yard cringing behind its wall for safety – afraid to venture out – while kids already on the outside were obliged to scramble up side streets or into doorways for protection from the next tear-gas attacks – which seemed almost certain to come.

And they did at about 7:30 when the crush of school kids being frantically urged out of the area by their teachers was encountering a reverse wave of still arriving youngsters – unaware of what had been happening. Suddenly a Jeep careened from around a corner, sped through the scrambling swirls of excitable and worried boys and girls clear to the other end of the long block, but then came to a sudden, sliding stop.

Shrieking kids, already scampering to get out of the way and sensing what was about to happen next because of years of similar never-ending, always unsettling experiences, started running even harder to stay clear. Inevitably a tear-gas canister was sent flying their way. It clattered onto the street near a group of quickly scattering children: its white sinuous snake-like smoke issuing forth in a steady, ominously hissing stream, which then quickly plumed into a wispy cloud enveloping several youngsters who dashed out of the foggy pall holding their hands to their noses as they ran.

Then two more canisters were fired from the opposite direction. As one plopped out of the sky, its contents already spewing forth–this time like a fleecy sausage–one youngster dashing from upwind snatched up a canister and threw it clear of the kids into whose midst it had fallen...back towards the Jeep.

Good try.

But it landed closer to me, and then I proceeded impulsively to do one of the dumbest things I've done in a long time. Being upwind, I moved serenely and confidently closer to the canister to get a really neat close-up with my digital camera.

But then the wind shifted.

Meanwhile Kristin Anderson, looking to see where everyone had rushed to get out of the way, got too close to the advancing cloud and had her own uncomfortable wheezing, coughing, tear-streaming moments to work through.

Recovering, some of the CPTers regrouped outside the Marief School gate where the near-frantic headmaster asked them to help shepherd his students out of the schoolyard. As Anderson, Yoder, the headmaster and other teachers were leading a large contingent of kids out into the street, another speeding Jeep raced toward them. The CPTers and the headmaster, instead of scrambling out of the way, this time stuck to the middle of the road and advanced grimly toward the rapidly approaching Jeep, clearly refusing to flinch or get out of its way, while at the same time motioning–hopefully–for it to stop.

It did.

Moving to the window on the driver's side, they asked him to radio other Jeeps to stay away and call a halt to the tear-gassing so the adults could escort the children safely away from the area. The soldier agreed and in a few minutes the children were on their way to their homes without further interference from the Israeli army or border police.

As the crush of kids disappeared, Marief School's headmaster complained that since the start of the term at the beginning of September, his school had been closed down in a similar manner

20 times. Hebron Basic Boys School's headmaster told us that today's enforced closing was now number 15 for his school. Both said they feel the closures are a kind of deliberate provocation on the part of the soldiers and police to irritate the boys into throwing stones so that they will then have an excuse to retaliate against the kids even more violently, as well as have a rationale to keep closing down the schools.

We wondered: Was it a coincidence that curfew had been reimposed several minutes after the time Hebron's children normally head for school?

Meanwhile the anticipated 10,000 settler celebrants never showed up to commemorate Abraham's acquisition of Macpelah Cave and its adjoining field. The number was considerably less. No one in an official capacity is saying how many actually came, but some guess all that malign energy was expended on behalf of fewer than 3,000 visitors—pious yet militant so-called descendants of the founding patriarch on whom the irony of the situation is apparently lost. Year after year they still reverently commemorate Abraham's *scrupulous* purchase of the place a few thousand years ago, while they today are continuing their relentless, never-ending *theft* of the same area from its Palestinian inhabitants.

8

There Goes the Neighborhood

East Jerusalem, Palestine, December 4, 2002

A not particularly vast block of stone–but large enough–
stands at an Israeli military checkpoint in Hebron. It helps control
access to the area between the large settlement of secular and religious ultranationalist Jews on Hebron's eastern edge called Kiryat
Arba and the special security zone, established by Israel's Ministry
of Defense in the heart of Hebron's Old City. The security zone
surrounds the ancient Ibrahimi Mosque known in Israeli circles as
the Tomb of the Patriarchs.

On one side of the sentinel stone these words appear:

1. Life
2. Short
3. Years
4. What?
   ...Ira

The cynicism was probably inscribed one dreary day not too
long ago by a skeptical–or at least terribly confused–Israeli
sentry-soldier. Ever since the bloodletting events of Friday evening, November 15, I have been pondering Trooper Ira's words–
especially the last one: "4 What?"

For what indeed are those "3 Years" of mandatory military
service required of most young Israeli men and women?

Many people over here and back home are insisting the clearly brave Israelis who died in the fierce gun battle just down the hill from Kiryat Arba's southernmost entrance were killed in an unhesitating defense of their country. That would be true in a technical sense if one considers the West Bank and Gaza as de jure districts of the state of Israel. However, for those who view Israel's military rule over the territories as an internationally unsanctioned and unrecognized de facto condition – and therefore illegitimate – the best they can say is that those nevertheless fruitless Israeli deaths were incurred not in defense of their country but on behalf of a colonialist ideological tail – wagging a virtually helpless dog – one that has been and is being hemmed in by cold and equally unyielding ideologues.

And "4 What?"

Contrary to first reports in the domestic and international press, no unarmed civilians were killed or wounded or came under attack. Kiryat Arba's Friday evening worshippers on November 15 had already been escorted safely back home [Ed: See next report for fuller description of the ambush]. So complaints of terrorism don't hold water; most of the Israeli causalities were either soldiers or border police returning from their successful mission of protection. However, given the axiom concerning the staying power of first dispatches from the field, Benjamin Netanyhu is having his way; and the skirmish is being remembered massively as a "massacre" of unarmed worshippers by terrorists instead of another clash of the military with guerrillas, which even Ariel Sharon admits it was.

So "4 What?"

Sharon, now in the midst of a reëlection campaign, can afford to be big about the difference, because the episode has provided him with a potentially powerful vote-winning opportunity to initiate a personally touted land-grab scheme in Hebron, which, although hatched by him several years ago, nevertheless has needed a big pretext to get it going. Now he's got that.

Once it gets rolling it will involve a new wave of home demolitions and land expropriations. The result will be a significant leap in the spread of settlements within a to-be-established ulcer-like band of newly expropriated territory in the Old City, This will stretch westward along a route from Kiryat Arba's southern gate to the Ibrahimi Mosque/Tomb of the Patriarchs structure a quarter-mile away and then continue on from there for another half mile.

The enlarged Israeli area will absorb and more securely connect Hebron's ultranationalist inner city settlements to Kiryat Arba. Isolated behind high thick cement walls, the contemporary Carcassonne will swallow up scores of Palestinian apartments, homes and shops long coveted and repeatedly harassed by settlers who, more often than not, have been abetted by soldiers and police. The finished project will effectively divide a significant section of the Old City into a kind of Buda and Pest.

Again "4 What?"

Sharon has described the desired result of this scimitar-shaped multi-gated fortress community as providing the means for "contiguity" between the 6,000 residents of Kiryat Arba and the 450 residents of the several tiny inner-city settlements. Of course, throughout the rest of the West Bank and Gaza, Israel has created the opposite condition: a garroting-like non-contiguity between every Palestinian village, town and city – enforced and perpetuated by cement, boulder and earthen roadblocks intended to prevent unregulated entrance or exit. The barricades are augmented where and when necessary by the military.

Does anyone remember that Sharon's current highly and publicly valued notion of *contiguity* with respect to Jewish neighborhoods in the heart of Hebron contradicts Israel's stance at the Camp David negotiations in the summer of 2000? Back then, Israeli leaders, including Sharon as well as U.S. officials, were highly critical of Palestine generally and Yassir Arafat specifically for refusing to make even a counter-proposal to Israel's so-called "generous offer" of bits and pieces of non-contiguous land?

Finally "4. What?"

Ironically as far as many of the settlers of Kiryat Arba and the handful living in the center of the Old City are concerned, Sharon's dream is not theirs. They want the two districts enlarged and contiguous, all right, but they do not want the walls. In their view the walls will create an ironic and therefore unacceptable ghettoized condition, too reminiscent of recent and more ancient Jewish history. However, they would be happy to accept the creation of the Buda and Pest condition described above, minus the palisades, which would be replaced by human shields – several thousand more soldiers and border police assigned to protect them than are in the area now.

The goal of the Israeli force would be to banish Hebron's 150,000 Palestinians to their homes in what is becoming almost perpetual curfew. This curfew, by the way, means that school has been "out" for Hebron's education-starved youngsters ever since the attack and is not scheduled to resume until the end of the week. Food and other supplies have been running low. And hospitals and pharmacies have been difficult to reach.

In addition to those constraints and restraints (abetted by Sharon and the Israeli army despite the differences outlined above) Kiryat Arba's settlers have already been allowed by the Occupation's military rulers to establish and inhabit a heavily protected outpost on newly seized Palestinian land at precisely the spot where the Shabbat assault took place. Each day it is growing larger and considerably more ominous for Palestinian families living within its expanding orbit.

That sums up "4 What?"

Demolition orders have already been issued for the removal of at least ten homes standing in the way of the construction of the new walls. Some date back to the medieval era. So history as well as homes are on the verge of being unilaterally sacrificed in order to provide what is being described as a "promenade" for Kiryat Arba's orthodox worshipers, their religious practice dictating that they walk not ride during Shabbat.

Until now the word "promenade" has conjured up for me such blithe and nostalgically pleasant images as the Easter Parade; sun-drenched strolls on the Board Walk at Atlantic City or Central Park; elegant 19th century top-hatted and parasoled boulevardiers relaxing Seurat-like along the banks of the Seine, or Christopher Robin going down with Alice to view the always-festive, ceremonial changing of the guard at Buckingham Palace. So I simply cannot reconcile my understanding of the word "promenade" with Sharon's. The thought of anyone actually proceeding gaily along his new corridor–knowing that on either side of it other human beings are being obliged to live like caged animals in a sideshow–is, to say the least, unspeakably bizarre.

(TO BE CONTINUED)

9

Nights of the Furies

Ibillin, Galilee, Israel, December 12, 2002

At about 7:00 early Friday evening, November 15th, CPTer Mary Yoder and I passed through the always-guarded special security zone surrounding the Ibrahimi Mosque/Tomb of the Patriarchs. Suddenly they heard gunfire which seemed to be coming from not too far beyond the mosque in the direction of Kiryat Arba, the large settlement of ultranationalist and religious Jews situated about a half-mile away on the eastern rim of the city. Within seconds they heard answering shots, but louder, which meant the Palestinians had probably fired first and the military was firing back.

Suddenly four soldiers dashed tensely by in the direction of the shooting – their guns at the ready. "What's happening?" Mary called out, not really expecting an answer, but she got one from the soldier bringing up the rear. "Welcome to Hebron," the trooper muttered as he raced by.

Minutes later the CPTers reached the Christian Peacemaker Team apartment, where within an hour the first inaccurate reports from the field began to make their way on to the internet and broadcast outlets. Several worshipers, soldiers, border police and civilian armed security guards, it was being reported, had been ambushed, killed and wounded.

Early the next morning several CPTers went to the scene of the shooting and offered condolences to the many settlers gathering there and also to many of the soldiers and border police stationed in the area. Settler tempers naturally were short. When I said, "Shabbat Shalom," to one who was carrying his young son on his shoulders, he kicked me just below the knee. Coincidentally it was the same man who months ago had screamed at me: "Our God will kill your God!" [Ed: See chapter 2]. His reaction, however, was the only negative response that entire day to CPT's repeated words of empathy (except for some preadolescent settler kids who threw stones, but were finally shooed away by soldiers).

At midmorning, Amira Hass, the bold, blunt *Haaretz* correspondent who for many years has lived in, reported from and reflected in print on the debilitating impact of the occupation on the Palestinians, first in Gaza and now the West Bank, called to ask if CPT would accompany her to the shooting site in the afternoon. By mid afternoon they were back in time to hear an Israeli army officer explain to Israeli and international journalists that no worshipers had been killed because their military guards had already safely escorted them back to Kiryat Arba. However, armed civilian resident security guards racing to the sound of the first shots were among the dead and wounded. Clearly the ambush was a traumatic event for the military and the settlement, "We made many mistakes.... We lost control," the officer said.

While at the scene, a terrified Palestinian man whose home is at the side of the road leading from Kiryat Arba to the mosque and closest to the settlement's entrance – no more than 50 yards from it – asked CPT to spend the night with his family in order to try to discourage collective settler retaliation. Previously broken windows and bullet holes indicated that his worries were far from unfounded, and a large after-dark rally to take place about 50 yards further down the road had already been announced.

Three CPTers – Mary Lawrence, Greg Rollins and I – plus future CPTers John Lynes and Amira agreed to stay. At about 7:30, the rally began, attended by approximately 1,500 angry settlers and protected by a large contingent of soldiers, border police and civilian police. During the hour-and-a-half of speech making, some settlers broke away and stormed into a nearby Palestinian street, smashing car and truck windows and lights as they went.

Meanwhile Amira accompanied by CPT slipped from the Palestinian home and mingled in the crowd. Then as the rally began to break up, a group of increasingly agitated settlers began stoning the compound in which the worried family lived. In addition they created a terrifying racket by beating furiously on its metal garage doors. That's when Amira made a conscious decision – she explained later – to jettison her reporter status on behalf of the terrified Palestinians. Followed by the CPTers, she waded through the crowd to a police car parked in front of the compound and demanded they do something to stop the abuse.

Two police got out, not to interfere with the pelting and noisemaking, but to protect one of their own stationed in the midst of the crowd. At the same time, settlers who had heard Amira's demand for protective action suddenly began turning primarily on Amira and secondarily on her CPT associates, forcing them gradually against the outside wall of the compound.

For several minutes she bore the brunt of the settler rage and abuse. But all of them – Amira and the CPTers – were to varying degrees pummeled, spat on and screamed at. Naturally she was called a traitor and worse. Then one settler woman snatched her notebook. Someone else tore her glasses from her face. Furious voices repeatedly warned and ordered her and CPT to get out and stay out of Hebron. In answer, she yelled defiantly to the crowd that she wasn't going to leave until she got her glasses back. That being the case, neither was CPT.

Even though an army Jeep with its contingent of three soldiers who were watching the mob passively was parked across the road no more than 25 feet away, the path to this presumed sanctuary, due to the soldiers' diffidence, was blocked by the crowd. After about 15 minutes a big, strapping Israeli television reporter acquaintance of Amira's appeared. Attracting the mob's attention, he led the way commandingly to the Jeep – the settlers parting reflexively in front of him like the Red Sea before Moses.

As soon as they made it to the Jeep, the Red Sea closed in again. For the next two hours the abuse was no worse than angry epithets, threats, short-range spitting and a bit of pebble throwing, but there was no getting away. Finally police came and led them to the safety of a big police bus about 75 yards further down the road and well away from the rally site. Just before they left, a young army officer appeared and quietly passed a small plastic shopping bag to Amira. Untying it, she found not only her notebook but also her glasses – broken in two, but nevertheless safely back in her possession.

Because the too-large group of settlers still did not disperse, it was impossible to get back to the family inside the compound, but with the worst apparently over, they were able to reach the family's father via cell phone; he said he thought they would be all right for the rest of the night, which was the case. Well after midnight the weary five headed back to the CPT apartment.

Since then, CPTers have been asked to stay – and are staying – almost every night in the homes of those families who live in the shadow of Kiryat Arba and who still fear, with good reason, settler and military reprisals.

10

Road Rage

Ibillin, Galilee, Israel, December 13, 2002

For more than a decade an astonishing if not unique remaking of the Palestinian map has been taking place. A succession of Israeli governments has been pursuing a massive bypass-highway-building campaign designed not only to remake the map of the West Bank and Gaza, but also, if not to remake history, at least to leverage it.

What were once main roads in the occupied territories no longer lead directly to, into and through the places where for centuries they traditionally led – ancient Christian and Muslim Palestinian villages, towns and cities. Now access to and from the smallest Palestinian hamlet to the largest municipality by means of those venerable thoroughfares, as well as other ancient roads and tracks, has been choked off by scores of checkpoints and barricades – augmented by constant curfews – all of which are intended to keep Palestinians in their place: out of sight, relatively speaking, if not out of mind.

Of course, the never-ending tit-for-tat violence – fomented, encouraged, rationalized and carried out by Palestinian radicals and the radicalized Israeli military – guarantees that Palestinians can never be out of mind, although Israeli officialdom keeps trying.

The new system of comfortably wide, blacktopped bypass highways has been planned to skirt the Palestinian reality by providing
direct (and therefore presumably safer) access to the ever-encroach-
ing Jewish settlements in the West Bank and Gaza. Over the decades these settlements through legalistic subterfuge, downright
seizure, confiscation and nighttime stealth have been erected systematically and relentlessly on the sites of former Christian and
Muslim Palestinian homesites and farmlands.

Gertrude Stein once expressed this indelible thought: "There
is no there...there." A century ago modern Zionism's founders
became the propagators of a myth that the *there* of Palestine was
a land without a people waiting for a people without a land. In
other words there were no Arabs *there*. Then a generation back,
Israeli Prime Minister Golda Meir gave a new twist to the notion –
when it had become abundantly clear to the entire world that
there were and had always been plenty of Palestinians...*there*. Repeatedly she tried to convince world opinion there were no such
people as Palestinians *there*. That verbal sleight of hand did not
prevail either. Since then, Israel's road builders in the territories
have been hard at work helping to perpetuate a condition in
which there will be increasingly less of a there *there* for the Palestinians than for the settlers; less of a there *there* to be put back
under Palestinian administration or an eventual contiguous Palestinian sovereignty.

The West Bank and Gaza are the only places in the world I
know where an extensive and extremely demeaning set of *us*-again-
st-*them* roadways is being constructed – glaring examples of some
of yours and my apparently fungible tax dollars at work with loan
guarantees and outright grants. These continue to perpetuate Israeli
domination and diminution of Palestinian (Christian and Muslim)
culture, society, politics and presence. Someday – perhaps sooner
rather than later – if the Palestinian *there* continues to shrink, will
the only facts on the ground in the West Bank be a totally Israeli
there *there*?

In fact, with respect to the shrinking Palestinian land area, even though the focus is mostly on the settlements, the new road system has consumed much more of the land – about 17 percent – than the settlements and much of this had been agrarian because the bypass roads shun built-up Palestinian areas and instead deliberately circumvent them. As a result the new roads have taken a huge bite – thousands of *dunams* (each a quarter of an acre) out of once-productive land, which in all likelihood is gone for good.

The connecting highways inside Israel, just as much as the bypass roads and settlements, have also become bleeding symbols of the out-of-control hatred and rage that – in the form of violence and counterviolence – has become the characteristic of Intifada II resistance and counter-resistance; for it is on or along highways and lesser streets in both Israel and Palestine that so many of the killings take place. These in turn are the most memorable manifestation of Israeli and Palestinian pain turned to rage.

All roads are potential conduits or locales for the never-ending reflexive violence. The Israelis use the roads baldly to scurry their troops, tanks and other military vehicles from one "danger zone" to another in order to cow and terrorize the civilian population. Meanwhile young Palestinians are furtively sneaking along many of those roads in order to kill in an exceedingly indiscriminate manner and also with the aim of cowing and terrorizing civilians.

The Israelis and Palestinians engaged in terror are not entitled to claim they are involved in either legitimate armed struggle or legitimate self-defense. Notwithstanding the uneven level of the sophisticated armaments possessed by Israel contrasted to the essentially pop-gun nature of the Palestinian arsenal, this disparity in fire power does not provide a moral rationale for some Palestinians' resort to the suicide card.

Tragically, channeled Palestinian youngsters are being enticed to turn themselves into deadly (but culpable) smart bombs or mini-F-16s in order to administer a brand of outrageous collective punishment that is just as contemptible and counterproductive as that being meted out by Israeli soldiers and border police. The troopers excuse their behavior by claiming they are just doing their duty, even though they too are being tragically maneuvered into furthering official policies of revenge. All this leads to social and political debilitation, additional land expropriation (masquerading as security measures) or disingenuous invitations to further violence.

Yesterday two more soldiers doing their duty on guard near the Ibrahimi Mosque in Hebron's Old City were killed by Palestinian guerrillas. One was the first Israeli female conscript to die in combat during the current uprising. They were killed by snipers hidden along the same road quite close to the spot in Hebron where twelve soldiers, border police and armed civilian security guards were ambushed the middle of last month. Reprisals – which will be deemed doing "one's duty" – can be expected.

However, does the following story qualify as simply doing one's duty?

One day a jitney full of Palestinians and I were making the slow 20-mile trip from Hebron to Jerusalem. We were stopped for the inevitable security check by Israeli soldiers at a roadblock. After glancing at my passport and realizing that not only was I an American but also my last name was Levin, he asked me angrily, waving deprecatingly at my fellow passengers, "Is this your family?"

Instead of answering, I /quietly asked, "Why not?"

My fellow Palestinian passengers held their breaths.

Instead of answering me, he shouted back even more angrily and insistently, "Is this your family?!?"

This time, I answered, "Of course," but then added, "Why, isn't it yours?

He did not answer, but instead disgustedly flipped my passport back at me, dumped the rest of the ID's into the lap of a Palestinian and waved us on – my fellow passengers high-fiving me as we drove away.

11

The Dying Stones

The first time I heard anyone make a plea on behalf of the "Living Stones" of the Holy Land was in the mid-1980s during one of the trips Sis and I made to the region as members of a series of fact-finding delegations. The aim was to observe and comprehend firsthand and up close conditions of life – or lack thereof – in the West Bank and Gaza.

It could have been Mar Elias Educational Institution's founder Abuna Elias Chacour from whom we heard it first, or Sabeel Ecumenical Liberation Theology Center founder Reverend Naim Ateek, or human rights advocate Jonathan Kuttab, or perhaps someone else – I am not sure anymore. Who said it, is the not the point. What they said is.

It is not enough – they emphasized back then and during the increasingly bitter years which followed – to come to the Holy Land to examine the inert remnants of the past, its "Dead Stones" comprising crumbling, religious and secular edifices of antiquity, or the only slightly less ancient medieval- and post-medieval sites, monuments and artifacts. More important for people passing through, they urged, would be to visit, observe and come to understand the Holy Land's "Living Stones" which are the descendants of the past, the human flesh and blood remnant still hanging on here perilously in the present. The human context of the *Dead Stones*, they argued, can only be understood – and the terrible conditions can only be transformed – when the dreadful conditions of the *Living Stones* of today have been acknowledged and effectively communicated.

Although this has been relevant for the precipitously shrinking Arab-Christian population of Palestine and Israel, it is of equal importance to Muslims here, too, as well as to the steadfast Israeli Jews who over the years have been struggling in Israel as well as in the occupied territories to alleviate the suffering and raise the visibility of the debilitating cultural, social and political forces cruelly baffling and ruining the lives and livelihoods of their Arab neighbors. So these articulate and eloquent Palestinians wanted to impress us that what is needed was a concerted effort to convince the multitude of would-be travelers to the area to do more than eyeball the *Dead Stones* and then, calling it a day, head home.

This is what compels observer/activists from overseas to continue the efforts we have been making. Our voices, then and now, although dedicated, have been few, ignored and often ridiculed. Unfortunately those committed to the task have never constituted the critical mass needed to help foster a change in the itineraries of the main body of those visiting the Holy Land.

Tourism, which has accounted for most of the visitors to the region and which flourished until the violence and counter-violence of the current uprising killed it off, never met the challenge or the need of helping to preserve the *Living Stones* because the many visitors coming to the region with the multitude of so-called sacred tours of the Holy Land were mainly interested in seeing the historical *Dead Stones*. Suggestions – often pleas – to do otherwise met with only limited success, if not downright indifference or hostility. Consequently, few of those flocking to the *Dead Stones* of Israel, the West Bank or Gaza for an untroubled, inspirational holiday have detoured down that critical other road, either because they were unaware of its existence or by design.

Most sacred Holy Land tours are antiseptically planned so as to funnel pious sightseers only to the dead vistas and venues of yesteryear. Tour packagers have meticulously steered their devout charges away from potentially distasteful, distressing, eye-opening scenes that would give them politically, culturally or theologically challenging experiences with the *Living Stones*–those marginalized Palestinians and their Israeli partners struggling to survive and resist the confiscatory and demeaning occupation of the West Bank and Gaza. Avoiding the Palestinian reality in homes, refugee camps, villages, towns and cities, ostrich-like tourists to the Holy Land tend to perpetuate the grave international, experiential void. How sad that this remarkable opportunity to do otherwise has been lost.

Of course, the pleasure, awe, inspiration and excitement of journeying to the inanimate venues of the *Dead Stones* where so many consequential beliefs originated should not be avoided. The attraction of the *Dead Stones* is understandably important to the tourist trade in both Palestine and Israel. Ironically, since distances, relatively speaking, are minimal in the Holy Land one does not have to detour far off the beaten path leading to the *Dead Stones* to encounter the reality of the misery of Palestine's *Living Stones*. However, given the endurance and persistence of the violent colonialist and nihilist mentality found in varying degrees amongst both Israelis and Palestinians, which too many travelers to the area assiduously avoid, using the terms "Holy Land" and "Living Stones" has basically come to be an exercise in naïve nostalgia and futile longing.

Currently the "Holy Land" encompasses an unholy magnitude of death and despair among the so-called *Living Stones*. Due in part to a failure to motivate the urgent need for people outside the region, especially the United States, to come, see, comprehend and ultimately identify with the plight of all the *Living Stones* now in the West Bank and Gaza–and even, one can claim, of those in Israel–the more appropriate term would be to call them the "Dying Stones" of the not-so "Holy Land."

Dying Stones are the norm here now – the defenseless children and adults in both Palestine and Israel who have become the predictable and unwilling victims of the no-end-in-sight violence, of the vicious cycle of resistance, oppression and inevitable revenge by both the oppressor and the oppressed. The *Dying Stones* today are the increasingly radicalized young but lethal Palestinian slayers of the unarmed and their equally young Israeli conscript counterparts gunning down civilians, each of whom has been persuaded of the necessity to take leading roles in the existentially illogical bloodletting that leads absolutely nowhere.

Despite the reality of the *Dying Stones*, one of their most incredible and inspiring traits, which continues to astonish us despite the fact that we encounter it every day, is their capacity for hope. These amazingly resilient Palestinian and Israeli human beings, cling, it seems to me, beyond all logic and comprehension and current signs to the contrary, to hope and continue to trust that enough people to make a difference will – despite the risk, the cost and even their skepticism or bias – decide to come here long enough to experience and comprehend the terrible truth of the *Dying Stones*.

In the past the powerful example of such deserving hope has brought the dying and the dead back to life. It can happen again.

12

Supposing Everything West of the Mississippi Was Palestine

Old City, East Jerusalem, Palestine, January 6, 2003

As the year 2003 begins, Israel is pushing full speed ahead on one of its most astonishing unilateral actions to date. It is working furiously on a vast construction project that will effectively take many square kilometers of Palestinian land off a future negotiating table by building a very high barrier that it is calling a *separation* or *security fence*. For the most part it is being built well inside the Green Line that has marked the border between Israel and the West Bank since 1967.

How to describe the geographic, political and economic impact of this latest unilateral action? Just suppose everything west of the Mississippi – proportionally speaking – was the "West Bank" of Palestine and everything east of it was "Israel." If you flew over this area you would find an impenetrable barrier being erected many, many miles west of the Mississippi, deep inside "Palestinian" territory. When finished, all of Iowa, Missouri, Arkansas and parts of Minnesota and Louisiana will be annexed safely inside "Israel" without benefit of negotiations.

If you are having some difficulty perceiving the significance of the analogy, think "wall" and not "fence." *Fence* is an Israeli euphemism for the 25-foot-high barrier, which in many places will be thick concrete – top to bottom – and in other places a concrete base topped by an electrified fence. Imagine that and you can grasp why Palestinians are calling the new barrier a "Wall of Hate" or an "Apartheid Wall" – the existence of which will swallow up a critical slice of Palestine's most productive agricultural land. This land has been owned, tilled, tended and harvested by Palestinian farmers for centuries; but since work on the wall began last summer, an increasing number of farmers have been denied access to their assets. So the process of de facto annexation of this part of Palestine into Israel proper is already under way.

As we all know, even before construction on the wall began west of the "Mississippi," Israel had already established in every area of Palestine (in defiance of current international norms and agreements), more than a hundred post-1967 settlements comparable to Rochester, Moorhead and Minneapolis, Minnesota; Ames, Council Bluffs and Davenport, Iowa; St. Louis, St. Joseph and Poplar Bluffs, Missouri; Fort Smith, Texarkana and Hot Springs, Arkansas; and Baton Rouge, Lake Charles and Shreveport, Louisiana and, of course, more settlements further west than that – all the way to the Pacific. Soon all these cities in Iowa, Missouri and Arkansas and some in Minnesota and Louisiana will no longer be settlements in Palestine, but municipalities in Israel.

Their settler inhabitants naturally will continue to have all the rights of Israeli citizenship. However, even though Israel's current Palestinian population has legal second-class-citizenship status, the west of the Mississippi Palestinians, who before long will find themselves trapped on the Israeli side of the wall, will not have even those rights. As a result, they will soon constitute a new and special case in statelessness, helplessness and hopelessness.

Furthermore the wall is being so craftily planned and laid out as to cut off Palestinian villages, which will not be annexed, from their adjacent fields and orchards – making those areas easy and inevitable targets and prey for expropriation by nearby Israeli settlements. Virtually all of the wall will be dug out of some of the most fertile vegetable tracts and fruitful orchards in the West Bank, despoiling them with a corridor about half-a-football-field-length wide. Often another 50 yards or more on one side – or both – is used to dump spill from the leveling-off process. Thus tens of thousands of *dunams* are in the process of disappearing beneath the concrete and wire – removed forever from cultivation.

The exact route of this approximately 220-kilometer-long barrier keeps shifting to accommodate vote-powerful settler blocs anxious during the current parliamentary election campaign to snatch more land from Palestinian control while they have the electoral clout. Current estimates – by both Palestinian and Israeli organizations monitoring the construction – are that around ten percent of the total West Bank area will be confiscated or destroyed. Besides valuable farmland and orchards, Israel will be making off with Palestinian water. Scores of groundwater wells will end up in Israeli territory and be lost permanently to Palestinian use.

To take one concrete example: The eventual wall in the Qalqilya district of the West Bank – about half of Missouri in our analogy – is going to be decimated and plundered by the wall so that 22 groundwater wells will disappear behind it; 25,000 fruit-bearing trees producing approximately 2.5 million boxes of oranges, lemons, and other citrus each year will be isolated from their Palestinian owners; 80,000 fruit and almond trees yielding 2 million boxes; 2,000 greenhouses producing 3 million boxes of vegetables; 4,000 *dunams* of fields yielding another million boxes of vegetables; 120,000 olive trees producing 500 tons of oil; and 12,000 additional *dunams* of potential crop and pasture land – all these means for survival – will be lost to the Palestinian economy. And that's just in the Missouri/Qalqilya District.

A few days ago, a farmer standing in the middle of the recently bulldozed corridor, which had destroyed dozens of *dunams* of his holdings and also sliced right through it, told how for several weeks he has been prevented from working his land on the Israeli side of the cut. He said at one point local Israeli officials, tired of being petitioned by him to let him get to his field, yelled, "You are a donkey!" The farmer answered back, "Only God can make a donkey and a man. Why are you trying to make me into a donkey?" Naturally, the farmer still can't get to his fields. "In every Palestinian house," he complained, "Sharon is making everyone crying."

As long as the effects of this new and extremely serious issue are disregarded or neglected in the West, Israel will be able to treat harshly and with impunity all complaints here about the wall, as it did a week ago in the town of Jayyous, which is in the process of having 75 percent of its farmland, orchards and all its current water resources disappear behind the wall. When a group of locals and internationals came down the hill from the town to the wall to stage a nonviolent protest, they were stopped by Israeli military and armed civilian security guards from a nearby settlement. After a quiet discussion, the group was told that it would be allowed to proceed in about 30 minutes. Some 20 minutes later, an army Jeep and a police Jeep rolled relentlessly down on the group from behind. Two soldiers burst from the Jeep brandishing stout batons. After a few seconds of angry shouting, one soldier fired off a percussion grenade. Others fired tear-gas canisters at the delegation. Then shots were fired by the Israelis.

Frustrated, angry boys began throwing and slinging stones back at the soldiers, while older Palestinian men tried to get the boys to stop but couldn't. The barrage of stone throwing, which continued for half an hour, was answered with intermittent retaliatory gunfire. One Palestinian was wounded. One was arrested. Then curfew was imposed and the demonstrators dispersed.

A few days later a similar event planned a few kilometers to the north in Tulkarm never got off the ground. The Israelis, perhaps getting wind of what was planned, declared curfew early that morning and dispatched extra forces to the area in order to keep things quiet.

13

Trusting God More and Our Military Less

Birmingham, Alabama, March 15, 2003

Our nation is on the verge of making a precipitous policy leap from containment and deterrence to waging preëmptive war against Iraq. Because of that possibility the Christian Peacemaker Team (CPT), in order to bear witness to God's boundless love for our threatened brothers, sisters and cousins there, has been standing with helpless Iraqi children, women and men who will inevitably be caught in the crossfire. Early next week Sis and I will be on our way to join and stand with them. We hope in our small way to help counter the hateful indifference to life that is putting them in harm's way: a hateful indifference exemplified by a concept, which has been bandied about lately—that of "necessary evil." In Iraq "necessary evil" will be further euphemized into "collateral damage," as it has been called for the past twelve years there.

But I cannot accept the notion of collateral damage—an essentially egocentric derivation of "necessary evil"—any more than the disingenuous concept that good can come from evil. The ideas of "necessary evil" and "good coming from evil" are the heart, or more accurately, the heartlessness, of the rationale used to justify the terrifying results of the all-out war the U.S. apparently is planning to wage against Iraq.

Good may come about *despite* evil, but the wicked, indiscriminate sowing of death, which is bound to happen in Iraq and that is happening every day in Palestine and quite often in Israel, is too high a price to charge those who have no say in how a struggle supposedly on their behalf is to be waged. Although Christians will tell you that Jesus died for all our sins, thousands of innocent Iraqi people with no place to hide soon may be made into sacrificial lambs dying for the sins of both Saddam Hussein and George Bush.

That must not happen.

Despite my objections to what I perceive as worrisome zealotry with respect to actions the United States is trying to launch, I nevertheless believe it is important to be loyal – loyal to the intent and universal appeal of the American dream – the American ideal – as expressed in the Declaration of Independence. That dream and its appealing ideals for too long have been turned inside out by too many of our leaders – perched on top of our social and political pyramid – and their elastic morality. They are intent on making the world safe – not just for democracy, it turns out – but also for tyrants and despots who accommodate our profligate and voracious consumer appetite for products, no matter what the impact is on the poor or oppressed.

So I am not convinced that this time we will get it right, because at the beginning of this new century the United States is picking up where it left off – seeking, as the president's national security memorandum put it, to enlarge the community of market economies by extending the benefits of freedom everywhere even if it takes a so-called preëmptive war to do it!

Presumably to further that policy, the U.S. is poised – despite repetitive polemics about democratic nation-building – to turn oil-rich Iraq into a modern-day equivalent of the many Central American banana-rich or coffee-rich oligarchies and other strategically significant nations elsewhere whose chances to become democracies too often over the past century were not really helped by our overt or covert violent interventions. So at a time when our nation should be examining and reëxamining its fears and trusting God with them more and our military with them less, we are on the verge of bombarding the Iraqis closer back to the Stone Age from which they may well have been the first people on earth to emerge.

With respect to our specific faith, Sis and I believe the times do not call for any more Christian soldiers; instead they cry out for Christian and other peacemakers like CPT who are willing to risk proactive nonviolence by standing in the way of violence. Sadly, such peacemakers are in short supply. This doesn't mean we should not support our young people – and the not so young – of our military. Given the mythological war-brings-peace drumbeat to which they are being inexorably ordered to march, they especially need our support. I think the best way to demonstrate our care for them is to tell our leaders: Don't do it! But if you are so intent on war, let George do it. By himself!

These days when I express such revisionist concerns about violence and war, I am inevitably challenged by some who will argue that nonviolence can never be a practical solution to the issues facing us right now, either as individuals or as a polity. My answer to this challenge goes something like this: Nonviolence has never really been given a chance to prove itself as a creative and altruistic alternative to war. Violence on the other hand has had a several-thousand-year head start to solve problems, yet it certainly hasn't proved either its practicality or feasibility. There is a huge qualitative and quantitative difference between *just peace-making* and so-called *just war* or *jihad* – and this difference is lives: not just the lives of the so-called bad guys but, equally important, the lives of so-called good guys too.

For arguments such as these to register nowadays, they have to penetrate the static created by charges of unamericanism, of being a Sadaam collaborator, of being treasonous and – because of the proximity of the Israel/Palestinian issue – of being anti-Semitic. Naturally, such charges are discomfiting, but we are reminded that

God's love is for everyone, even for those who belittle our motives and try to stampede us into silence and inaction.

So – despite the barbs – we try to shrug them off. And we do that because, as my fellow hostage, Presbyterian missionary Benjamin Weir, once told Sis and me, "Being a peacemaker is never easy. But can you think of better work?"

14

Who Is Babylon?

Amman, Jordan, April 6, 2003

These days Ben Tre is very much on my mind, because Baghdad is. Sis and I and other members of CPT's presence in Iraq have just returned from Baghdad. Ben Tre was the city during the Vietnam War that an exulting U.S. military public information officer declared was destroyed in order to save it. The comparison may not be seamless but the similarities, if you can excuse the intended irony, are close enough for government work. Unfortunately, with respect to lunatic geopolitics, all of Iraq is on the verge of becoming like Ben Tre.

In testing homicidal technology (which is what military hardware is all about) Iraq is also terrifyingly comparable to the defenseless village of Guernica. It was there during the Spanish civil war that Fascist bomber pilots, warming up for what turned out to be the Axis' failed attempt to establish a "new world order" (ah there, George Bush Senior!), tested their attack techniques and weaponry and virtually obliterated the town. Pablo Picasso immortalized that calamitous event in his powerful neo-Goyaesque painting of the same name.

As our Iraq Peace Team delegation made its way out of Baghdad – Ben Tre – Guernica, Allied forces were closing in on it. The run-down city was hushed, uncertain and almost in a state of suspended animation. The effects of the previous war, followed by years of sanctions and blockade, and now the new war with its intermittent but round-the-clock air raids had brought the normal city hustle and bustle to a halt. People were hunkered down safely – they hoped – behind closed doors and shuttered or taped windows. Most shops not related to daily survival – such as food stores – were closed. Traffic was moderate, making Baghdad appear to be on the verge of becoming a ghost town. Hovering over the buildings a black smudge-like haze permanently shrouded most of the city, the result of a series of burning trenches of oil encircling the area. They had been kept blazing since the war began in a futile gesture to obscure potential targets from the Allies' shock-and-awe air raids.

We nonviolent humanitarian communicators and the international press still operating in Baghdad could occasionally still encounter ordinary citizens when our Foreign Ministry "minders" took us to see and gather firsthand accounts of the toll in lives and lingering pain the bombings were taking in demonstrably civilian areas. People from the neighborhoods affected would be on hand as we pulled up in cabs driven by government-approved drivers.

Survivors were anxious to tell their stories of suffering and fear, expressing bewilderment and rage over why they were being made to pay such a steep price for the actions of a government over which they had no control. They were angry not only that they were being hit instead of military or other strategic areas that contribute to official belligerence and resistance, but also because increasing evidence indicated anti-personnel fragmentation devices were being dropped on them. These weapons are designed to maim and wound, not necessarily destroy. From a distance a person struck by these solid metal, sharp-edged flying shards looks like someone with a bad case of the measles; close up the "measles" turns out to be bleeding wounds from which removing each jagged pellet is inevitably painful and difficult.

If the purpose of this aspect of the Allies' air campaign was to create docility among the populace in Baghdad toward the invasion and a spirit of revolt against the Iraqi police state, it appeared to be having an opposite effect. An unanticipated byproduct of the rising civilian death toll was a growing anger against the Allied fomenters of this war being waged against helpless and uninvolved Iraqis. We also observed an increasing iconization of Saddam Hussein in the very center of what was still his nation—a process which may only have served to harden the resolve and nerve of this anti-heroic strongman's increasingly beleaguered regime and life. This is not to say his regime will not fall, for there is the strong probability of this happening. However, there is also the likelihood of the aftermath turning out like Afghanistan's with its increasingly hollow victory for the U.S., not to mention for the millions of Afghanis living uneasily outside the safety of the small enclaves protected by our forces.

Democracy in much of Afghanistan is a mere slogan. So-called "liberated" Afghanis are having to cope with living in violently unstable areas run by warlords. In view of this lack of genuine success by the regime change, there is much to be said for the notion that when it comes to establishing democracy Allied leaders need to learn to crawl before deciding to walk. Or is our nation going to keep up our historically calamitous practice—for many of the vulnerable peoples we profess to be setting free—of violently attempting to update our convictions concerning Manifest Destiny and the arrogant perquisites of superpowerism? Are we going to keep at that no matter how many innocents die as we relentlessly seek to fulfill our so-called "patriotic duty" and resolve to "liberate" and spread democracy?

Just before the last Gulf War, I was on a panel with some theologians who certainly could recite many more scripture verses than I can. We were trying to understand the battle taking place in scriptural terms. I still can remember one scholar who was on the side of leveraging the End Times, saying, "Up to now I had always thought that all those prophecies concerning Babylon had to do with Rome. Now I can see, they really meant Baghdad."

To which I barely resisted blurting out, "Make up your mind!" For the question remains, "Who is Babylon?" Afterwards I reread Habakkuk looking for an answer. If you read chapter two, even if religious conviction is not your thing, you'll see that the prophets had ways of describing the human condition that stand the test of time. Here's one sample: "You have plundered the people of many nations, but now those who have survived will plunder you...because of the violence you have committed against the people of the world and its cities." Does that shoe fit?

So the vision I have these days of Babylon and its fall is not so much of Baghdad – whose imminent fall certainly will bear some resemblance to that ancient event – but more like the fall of the World Trade Center. The potentially apocalyptic significance of that stupefying event we are continuing to ignore and deny at the entire world's peril.

15

Where Have All the Lovebirds Gone?

Amman, Jordan, April 10, 2003

At dawn Thursday near the Jordanian border town of Ruwei-shed, the huge refugee tent cities readied for an influx of thousands of dispossessed Iraqis remained almost empty.

At least for the time being.

It is too soon to know whether the vast humanitarian crisis foretold by international relief specialists will cause defenseless Iraqis to ride out at home the hard-to-predict aftermath of the Allied invasion and the first days of a U.S.-run occupation or instead take flight to Jordan or Syria.

Given the sudden collapse Wednesday of the central government in Baghdad, a decision to cut and run will depend on what additional storms of violence and looting plus shortages of food, potable water and medical supplies may be in the offing. It is an enormous task to try to meet the needs of a nation suddenly without an infrastructure, not to mention supplies. Despite the efforts of the occupiers, the nation declines swiftly into civil war.

A convoy of over a hundred international journalists – especially TV and wire services – who had been waiting impatiently for the first opportunity to join their stranded colleagues in Baghdad, was among the first to stream out of Amman toward Iraq late Wednesday night, all hoping to enter Iraq without benefit of visas; the Iraqi embassy in Amman had been denying them visas since before the war began. Without waiting for another turndown, the newsies simply took off not knowing what to expect at the border. Would they be allowed to leave Jordan when they did reach the border? And, if permitted to leave, would they find the Iraqi border station still staffed? Or would it be deserted?

Arriving before dawn Thursday morning, they found the border station still intact and they were refused entrance. By early afternoon Thursday the caravan, which had swelled considerably, was still stymied. Only a few made it past the Iraqi immigration building, where the three pictures of Saddam Hussein (one in a tailored blue suit, another in traditional Arab garb and the third in military uniform) for more than two decades had been one of the first sights to greet those trying to enter the country.

Back in Amman, the Jordanian government posted heavily armed security guards around the Iraqi embassy in response to telephoned threats the jittery staff had received. Mindful of what happened Wednesday at the long-closed Iraqi mission in London which had been broken into and looted, the young Jordanian officer in charge of the armed chaperons told me, "We are here because we must help them. They are our brothers."

The question for those of us still in Amman and anxious to get back into Iraq was: Would the embassy be open for business Thursday? It did open on time under the continuing protection of those Jordanian guards, but internationals seeking visas, including humanitarian volunteers such as our small Christian Peacemaker Team, a five-person contingent, were being turned away. The reason, according to a tired, bewildered and depressed embassy contact who in the past had helpfully facilitated hard-to-obtain permissions to enter Iraq, was because, "We have no one to talk to in Baghdad. We worry about the road. We cannot be sure it will be safe. And we do not know if we even have a job and authority at this moment. So, I think, we cannot let you in."

So those of us who had been in Baghdad after the war began, but who had to come out a few days before the curtain rang down Wednesday on 24 years of police state rule, are trying to assess at a distance the significance of both the jubilation and the looting – especially in the cities – that we have been witnessing on both Arab and English-language television. The joy in the Kurdish north, the Shiite south and Shiite neighborhoods in Baghdad is comprehensible. The Kurds and the Shia combined have been the oppressed majority in Iraq for decades, so their relief comes from their touching belief that they have indeed been liberated. The jubilation in the equally oppressed Sunni branch of Islam, from which the nominally devout Saddam Hussein sprung, is perhaps a bit more complex. Besides presumable happiness at the prospect of living in a less autocratic environment, they are also clearly ecstatic at not being among the over 1,250 civilians killed and 5,100 wounded by Allied air raids and fighting on the ground since the war began March 20th.

When our CPT delegation was in Baghdad, we had visited civilian neighborhoods hit with cluster bombs which on impact spew forth a blizzard of jagged projectiles whose only purpose is to pepper their civilian victims with multiple bleeding wounds. Those certainly are going to be almost impossible to forget. Outside one shattered shop along a main thoroughfare hit by two such bombs, I came across a victim desperately holding open his shirt so my colleagues and I could see and make note of what had happened to him and his hapless neighbors. On the ground at his feet was a birdcage with two sets of lovebirds inside – each set perched on its own little swinging bar. Instead of the birds cuddling up to each other in typical lovebird fashion, all four were sitting warily – it seemed to me – as far from each other as their perches allowed, exuding alienation and mistrust. Surely they weren't blaming each other for the chaos around them, but I suspect that in a world where cluster bombs exist to shock and awe, they are a paradigm for all in Iraq who must be careful and wary where trust is concerned.

This somehow explains the everyone-for-themselves looting now underway: the clearest indication of disintegrating order and the deterioration of interpersonal confidence, especially in the cities of a devastated Iraq. As a result, Allied forces are going to have to figure out how to control the looting and its attitudinal fallout, and then how to end it. But they need to accomplish this critical task quickly. If not, the historically divisive forces in Iraq, described earlier, could catch on to the fact that – despite the occupation and U.S. notions concerning regime change – what's left of the nation is in reality up for grabs.

16

Robbing the Cradle

Amman, Jordan, April 16, 2003

During the first days of the invasion of Baghdad, while Allied military forces were massively and exclusively protecting the Oil Ministry building plus the Palestine Hotel where the occupation administration had established itself, the soldiers and marines were protecting little else. As a result widespread looting took place at nearly every other critical institution in the city. Of course, there weren't enough occupation forces to do the policing necessary to prevent the looting, but the priority of choices initially made about what to protect did furnish credibility, I think, to the oft-heard charge that the invasion had more to do with "It's the oil, stupid," than with liberating the Iraqi people, which now appears to have been a means to that primary goal.

Way down the list, it seems, was protection for Iraq's celebrated collections of cultural and historical artifacts going back to the beginnings of agrarian and urban society. Yet there was common knowledge that obsessively acquisitive forces in the cutthroat world of antiquity collectors and dealers in the U.S. and elsewhere had designs on the tens of thousands of precious and irreplaceable items in those collections. There had even been an ad hoc group of acquisition-minded souls and potential artifact negotiators in the

U.S. who had lobbied officials to get behind an effort to sabotage Iraq's tough laws and regulations, now being ignored, about retention of its cultural and historical heritage.

As if on cue, on April 12th among the first unprotected buildings looted in Baghdad was the National Archeological Museum – the day after UNESCO's (United Nations Educational, Scientific and Cultural Organization) director general, Koïchiro Matsuura, sent a letter to American officials emphasizing the need to protect this building and other collections. He also pointed out that governments neighboring Iraq had urgently requested assurance that stolen objects would not pass beyond Iraq's borders into the hands of would-be acquirers. In addition, international police and customs officials, including INTERPOL, had been alerted to ensure that international conventions prohibiting cross-border trafficking in stolen artifacts would be enforced.

Speaking to reporters two days ago in Amman, UNESCO's Colin Kaiser said that based on his knowledge of behind-the-scenes pressuring in the U.S. during the buildup to the war, he felt that although the looting was "possibly spontaneous," his "suspicion" was that the "looting was organized." He asserted that since crucial museum inventories turned up missing along with tens of thousands of artifacts, his doubts had been confirmed. He also mentioned that earlier this month a letter had gone to Colin Powell, U.S. Secretary of State, officially alerting him to the impending cultural crisis. Kaiser said that he was unaware of any official reaction.

In order to play catch-up, UNESCO is organizing a high-level meeting tomorrow at its Paris headquarters. World-class Iraqi and international antiquities experts will meet behind secure doors to begin a preliminary assessment of the losses and determine what urgent steps are needed to protect collections still intact in Iraq and strategize how to get back at least some of the massive missing treasures. Robbing what has been called "the cradle of civilization" – where writing, law, sophisticated art, not to mention imperial warfare, began – of the objects and documents that constitute its rightful heritage is a dreadful crime to UNESCO, which has spent 25 years spearheading efforts to help Iraq safeguard and uncover its ancient heritage.

The question remains who ultimately is going to succeed: UNESCO and Iraq or the underworld characters trafficking in those myriad stolen treasures.

17

Bush Broke it. Why Doesn't He Fix it?

Baghdad, Iraq, April 22, 20023

Heavy traffic and getting heavier is back on Baghdad main streets. This is really not a sign that life is getting back to normal, but merely that the air and ground war is over – as well as the looting and institutional rampaging which kept most people indoors afraid to venture out for weeks. "It's the difference between night and day," my former CNN colleague Peter Arnett chortled to Sis and me when – after many years – we stumbled into a reunion while walking through the lobby of the hotel housing much of the international press. "Remember how it was during the last days of the regime and in the war?" Peter asked rhetorically. "We couldn't go anywhere without our 'minders.' Now everyone can go anywhere we want."

However, except to visit friends and family, for many of those Iraqis now able to go anywhere they want, it's a case of being all dressed up with no place to go – and nothing to do. No sight worth seeing is intact because of the air war and subsequent ground-war bombardments. There are still few jobs to travel to because, until today when power was restored – but only momentarily (not even long enough to boil water) – there has been no electricity with which to run the electronic technology and operate the simpler mechanical contrivances, which along with oil, had produced much of the nation's wealth and capital. The resulting relative prosperity had made Iraq, except for the dictatorship, one of the most sophisticated, better educated, as well as hygienically and medically better-off societies in the Middle East.

For several weeks there has been no electricity to light Iraqi homes or power domestic appliances which, even with the twelve long years of war waged against them by the U.S. and Britain, had enabled Iraqis a still relatively comfortable way of life. The few Iraqis who can afford gas-powered generators continue to light their nights, preserve their perishables in refrigerators, and cook, wash and operate their radios and TVs, which during prewar days even the less well-to-do could take for granted. But nobody dares drink the scarce tap water without boiling it.

Why has it taken so long to restore power to Baghdad – if only for those few tantalizing minutes today? There has been no official explanation from occupation officials, who apparently are content to let restoration – slow as it is – speak for itself. The inference Iraqis have been drawing is that "America has been leaving it for us to do." As a result, restoring power is very much on Omar's mind these days. An exasperated unemployed electrical engineer now working fitfully as a taxi driver-interpreter, Omar complained, "Bush broke it. So, why doesn't he fix it?"

"How can we fix it? And with what?" a perplexed college student named Ali asked. He is not just eager to start earning a currently nonexistent living, but more basically, he is anxious to complete his education at Al-Mustansirya University, Baghdad's second largest. Doing so, unfortunately, is on indefinite hold. Besides the absence of power, the campus is a mess! Most classrooms, labs and administrative spaces are in shambles: torn apart, looted or trashed by rampaging civilians during the first days of the city's occupation.

Our tour of the campus was monitored and chaperoned by young men in casual civilian clothes wearing green armbands made of green rags, who also were sporting menacing automatic rifles.

Obviously present to keep order, they scurried furtively around corners when we tried to take their picture. Apparently they were providing security with the blessing of the officer in charge of two huge U.S. tanks stationed across the street from the main entrance to the campus, because he could easily observe the armed youths as they civilly queried each person who approached the gate. "Our rules of engagement do not apply to boys like them. They are here to keep order," the officer said, "so we don't disarm them."

"Are they students?" I asked Ali.

"No. They're from the mosque."

"Why the mosque?"

"The imam told them to come."

"Why the green arm bands?"

"They are Shia," said Ali, as he anxiously pushed me along in order to comply with the guard's soft but firmly voiced recommendation to keep moving and complete our tour as quickly as possible.

Meanwhile, in the sprawling, dusty, dirt-poor neighborhoods where Saddam Hussein did the least for the people, particularly the Shia, the lights remain permanently off at night; water taps are dry for days on end; and there is no medicine for even the simplest of ailments. So these Iraqis, naturally among the first to cheer the Allies as "liberators" when it was safe to do so, are becoming disillusioned with the virtually nonexistent pace of restoring power, water, medicine or jobs, as well as the prospect of a drawn-out process to acquire U.S.-bestowed permission to rule themselves. So these fuming millions are quickly forming into hitherto unimagined broad-based combinations. A multitude of political parties – perhaps as many as 20 and rising – are emerging too in this former one-party nation ruled by a single person. Potential party loyalists are being wooed by organizers with offers of regular stipends for their future votes and vote-getting efforts.

However, the development of one particular broad-based coalition – probably the largest in Baghdad – is more than political. This historically unique alliance has the potential of becoming a social and religious phenomenon as well as political powerhouse. Comprised of poor Sunni and Shiite Muslims, this partnership is being organized, pursued and promoted by already popular and influential local Sunni and Shiite clerics. The Shia apparently are the senior partner in this arrangement which is assertively militant and politically radical by Western and current Arab establishment standards.

The coalition's savvy religious leaders, like their colleagues in other Middle Eastern countries, are adept at organizing and providing the reliable social, health and educational services capable of winning to their political agenda the hearts and minds of their deprived beneficiaries. Currently they have joined together to push for a quick end to the occupation and, hopefully, the subsequent installation of an elected government that will function along pious Islamic lines.

Saddam Hussein kept this kind of alliance from forming during his paranoid reign by sowing suspicion of the Shiite majority among his minority Sunni. The widespread fear he promoted led, as he planned, to hatred-motivated dissension, which enabled large-scale violent governmental persecutions, especially in the south. Sunnis who saw through the subterfuge and resisted Sadaam's divide-and-rule strategy were dealt with in equally atrocious ways.

Recently we visited a former Baath Socialist Party (Sadaam's party) neighborhood office located in a building on Palestine Street, a major Baghdad boulevard. It had been commandeered by Shia in the area who turned it into a mosque. As in many other districts, the men there were encouraging others from the neighborhood to help find those who had been involved in the post-invasion looting, not to punish them, but rather to get them to respond positively to a joint plea by their Sunni and Shiite cleric-leaders to give back what they stole.

We were impressed to find many of the young men there wearing green armbands like the ones we saw embellishing the sleeves of the youthful security guards at the university. On the new mosque's roof, snapping smartly in the breeze and – one could sense – snapping proudly, was a green flag. A horizontal banner perhaps 20 feet long hung on a low wall outside the building. I asked one of the young men to translate it. "It says," he answered fervently, "there is only one force – the force of Islam."

"What makes this force?"

Pointing to his right hand, he said, "This is Shia." Next pointing to his left hand, he continued, "This is Sunni." Then, interlacing his fingers, he squeezed his hands together tightly and added with a blissful smile, "That be one big force." At that moment a grinning companion, who had been nodding affirmatively as his friend explained the significance of the banner, placed a fresh red chrysanthemum in my hand.

So these people, too, are part of the unending traffic snaking along Iraq's main thoroughfares. Unlike those essentially aimless Iraqis described at the beginning of this piece, these Iraqis know exactly where they are going – and they are in a hurry to get there.

18

A Tank Called "Hostile"

Baghdad, Iraq, May 2, 2003

Like warriors of old, U.S. soldiers assigned to tanks like to give their weapons names that are then stenciled – in large black, easy-to-read letters – on the right and left sides of the barrels of their vehicles' powerful cannon. The honor of actually choosing a name usually goes to the crew's "gunner."

There are probably as many reasons for each name as there are tanks in the U.S. arsenal. The meaning of "Courtesy of the Red, White and Blue" or "Camel Tow" seemed clear enough to me, but another name I saw on a tank standing guard just inside the entrance to the Republican Palace, one of Saddam Hussein's former palatial places of rest and work, suggested that I not make any assumptions about it, even though it bore the potentially revelatory title of "Astonish." So I asked the gunner if there was any special reason why he settled on that name.

"Not really," he answered amiably. "I got me a dictionary. Started at the front and kept going until I found a word I liked."

"Does it fit with what you are doing now?"

"I hadn't really thought about that. I just liked the name."

The soldier who named the first U.S. tank we encountered as we reëntered Baghdad on April 18 clearly had an attitude which was unambiguously written on the barrel of his gun: "Hostile."

"Okay, so that's an attitude," I thought, "but does that also express intention?"

Not much later another issue emerged when we encountered a tank whose inscription asked the worrisome question, "Where's da Bitches at?" Not able to find the author, I nevertheless believe that here we were encountering an adolescent or barely post-adolescent fantasy put stupidly into words – but no intention.

Such a message cannot be reassuring to Baghdad women, very few of whom are venturing from their homes these days because of their fear of looting, robbery and worse by their own men. "If the soldiers won't protect them," a brother of one college-aged woman worried, "Who will? My sister will not leave our house, unless I go with her."

Another time we glimpsed the barrel of a tank rumbling noisily down a main thoroughfare providing protection for one of the ubiquitous convoys moving warily – guns at the ready – which you see round-the-clock everywhere: hodgepodges of solemn humvees, severe armored personnel carriers, unyielding trucks, determined tankers and resourceful recovery vehicles that look as if they had been assembled by a committee, all escorted by these don't-tread-on-me tanks. This tank's name was "Agamemnon." There was no way I could stop the convoy to ask Agamemnon's gunner the reasoning behind his choice, so I could only wonder about the extent and bent of this gunner's erudition.

Who was Agamemnon to this person? A good guy or a bad guy? Was there a connection between Agamemnon's war and this latest mother-of-all-wars-of-liberation and the rationale/incident used to fan the flames of assertive militancy and eventual aggression in the days of Troy and right now? Did our modern gunner recognize the screaming subtext to the Agamemnon story regarding the futility of war and violence? One way or another both war and violence change lives inevitably for the worse – both for those who engineer it and those who are helplessly victimized by it.

I would have felt better about this choice if I knew it was irony driven. But I'll never know. I suspect that instead of thinking ironically about Agamemnon, the author shared the contemporary super-patriots' view of the War of 1812 hero Stephan Decatur whose legendary words are said to be, "Our country! In her intercourse with foreign nations may she always be right; but our country right or wrong." With that sort of ideological precedent as a prevalent superscription to U.S. history, the logic that followed inevitably almost 200 years later was and remains, "If you are not with us, you are against us."

The fallout from such reasoning has been – not necessarily in order of significance – 1) the emergence, I am told, of "liberty fries" in fast-food outlets across America and 2) an increasingly frustrated Iraqi population, many of whom now feel snookered by the propaganda campaign waged by the Allies during the buildup to the invasion that seemed to promise much in the way of quickly installing a new normalcy in return for Iraqi civilians (and soldiers) sitting on the sidelines during the fighting. As a result, most Iraqis, taking the propaganda promises as binding contracts, did sit it out.

The Iraqi assumption, inspired by Allied-propaganda, was that the occupiers would deal with their needs not just with promised professional nation-rebuilding aplomb but – more important than that – with dispatch. The occupiers, until now, have been proving they are much more professionally adept and efficient at the making of the war than at quickly solving the problems created by it. A characteristic of this failure is a detectable penchant for making excuses for the frustrating pace of repairing critical damage to Iraq's vital institutions – as well as its national psyche – instead of providing, as required, the wherewithal needed so the people of Iraq can pick up the ball of liberation and run with it.

Specifically, the lacking "wherewithal" remains 1) security: looting continues plus a new problem mushrooming out of control – the unexploded explosives left over from the Iraqi arsenal lying dangerously in the open all over the city exacting a terrifying rising toll of curious young people being wounded, maimed and worse after venturing into areas the military still have not closed off or even marked as dangerous; 2) reliable electrical power: vast sections of the city remain without it or running water; 3) water-purification, garbage-collection and sewage-treatment facilities remain inoperable, so dysentery and diarrhea-stricken children are flooding already overcrowded, understaffed and medicine-short hospitals; 4) education: some school grounds have been occupied by slow-to-leave U.S. soldiers intent on uncovering abandoned or craftily stashed weapons left behind by Iraqi military and paramilitaries, which Iraqi parents and educators claim is hampering their efforts to get schools up and running again; 5) a health and nutrition infrastructure: hospitals are still being attacked and looted of medicine and equipment while minimal food supplies remain out of reach of the city's poor; 6) wage-producing jobs for Iraq's willing and educated workers, especially in vital governmental ministries, where the good jobs, so goes the complaint, are given mainly to former Baath Party workers.

In trying to investigate these issues, one finds it increasingly evident that in respect to these urgent needs, the occupiers are proving themselves professionally (or is it reflexively?) adept at hiding out or passing the buck. Thus for the better part of April the military was not accessible or was unwilling to answer inquiries regarding these concerns raised by the handful of frustrated NGOs [non-governmental organizations] still in Baghdad. Finally by the end of the month the occupation began a daily forum – consisting of a gaggle of low-to mid-level officers – to discuss problematic elements of the occupation with the NGOs.

The loudest and clearest message to emerge from these meetings was that the occupiers do not acknowledge that fixing them is their job. More than once attendees were told it's up to the NGOs to resolve the current crises. Moreover, questions or statements concerning the intent or efficacy of occupation policy too often are met with suspicion bordering on paranoia, because the only accessible officers are at a stage in their careers where carrying out policy with as few waves as possible washing up the chain of command – for which they can be held accountable in a way that might cloud their performance evaluations – seems like a be-all, end-all for them.

"The generals make policy. We are just doing our duty," is mostly what we hear. In other words: Make war not love. One beating-around-the-bush officer said warily to me after I asked a simple question, "When I talk to you guys, I always worry whether my answer is going to come back to haunt me." Despite such responses, occasionally we get more encouraging glimpses into what might be termed "a more positive operative ethos" among the Allied military. One glimpse came from a soldier who looked carefully around before telling me, confidentially, "Look, if we can't do better than this and soon, the honeymoon for us is going to be over quickly. And when it does end," he continued – mixing his metaphors – "it will go off like a rocket!"

We keep hearing remarkable anecdotes. An Iraq Peace Team stalwart, Wade Hudson, said a veteran of the Allies' dash from Kuwait to Baghdad told him that during the entire campaign he couldn't bring himself to fire a single shot. The soldier told Wade that although it may have looked like he was participating in the shooting, he was only pretending.

Also encouraging – kind of – was a conversation I had with a member of the crew of another tank named "California Dreaming." "We had a job to do," the first lieutenant said, "but I didn't like a lot of it." When I asked him to clarify, he said, "Too often the wrong people die in these things. I'm stuck with the memory of the morning when we first reached Baghdad and were manning a checkpoint. An Iraqi family kept coming on to us. Maybe they did not understand we were trying to get them to stop, but our rules of engagement were to shoot anyone who wouldn't. But they kept coming.

"Despite our frantic efforts to try to get them to understand they needed to stop, they just kept coming. So I gave the order to

shoot, which we did; and an unarmed family – a woman and her
kids – were killed. All of them were killed. This happened earlier
at Un Qasr too: the exact same thing. I don't like having to live
with that."

"So now what?" I asked.

"Well, I know one thing. When I get home, I'm quitting the
army. I'm not going to volunteer to do this again."

"What will you do?"

"I'm going to be a man of peace from now on."

"Meaning?"

"I'm going to join the FBI."

19

Questions and Some Answers

Baghdad, Iraq, May 3, 2003

On April 27, fellow CPTer Stewart Vriesinga presented the following questions concerning occupation actions and policy to a low-level U.S. military spokesperson serving with the occupation in Baghdad – the only officer of any grade to whom CPT had thus far been given access. The next day he received replies which, along with the questions, can be found, without comment, below.

Regarding the responsibilities of the U.S. interim government:

• Is the interim government being set up by the United States planning to undertake the provision of essential services provided by the previous regime?

Answer: I don't have enough information to answer that.

• If not, to whom should Iraqis look to provide and administer essential services? (Please provide names and locations of organizations.)

Answer: A combination of U.S. and coalition forces, NGOs, IOs [international organizations], will provide essential services. Troops are assessing the needs, and the information is being passed up and down the chain of command.

• How long must Iraqis be prepared to wait before the provision of essential services is resumed?

Answer: Some are being addressed immediately, others will take more time.

Regarding the Sadaam government's food distribution program:

• About 70 percent of the population of Iraq relies heavily on a food distribution program which was, up until last month [March], administered by the previous regime. [UNICEF has described this program as both the largest and most efficient food-distribution program in the world.] This month's supplies were due to be distributed on April 12, but were not. Because people's reserve supplies are running low and because of the spoiling of frozen foods due to long and on-going interruptions in electrical services, a food crisis is emerging. So given that this food distribution was a governmental program and an essential service on which the majority of Iraqis continue to rely, does the U.S. interim government accept responsibility for the resumption of this food distribution program?

Answer: I cannot answer that question.

• In the face of an emerging food crisis, when can Iraqis expect the resumption of this food distribution program?

Answer: [The question was passed over since the previous question was not answered.]

• If there are no immediate plans to resume the food distribution program, where and to whom can Iraqis turn now to avoid increasing incidents of malnutrition and diarrhea? (Please provide names of agencies, locations and hours of operation of current emergency food distribution centers.)

Answer: Iraqis can turn to the Civil Military Coördination Center (CMCC) to have their immediate food needs met.

Economic crisis: The interruption of electricity and telecommunications, the lack of security and public safety, the loss of salaries for both private- and public-sector employees, the looting and burning of banks, the freezing of investment capital held in overseas accounts and the destruction of businesses have all contributed to an almost total stop of all economic activity. So, in the face of the resulting economic crisis:

• Who will provide destitute and increasingly desperate Iraqi families with a subsistence income? When and where can they receive such an income?
Answer: I have no knowledge about that.

• Who will pay the salaries of Iraqi civil servants, private-sector employees and provide income to small businessmen who cannot return to work and provide their families with the basic necessities of life?
Answer: We are accepting job applications. We accepted applications for two days last week and will do so for three days this week. We can process about 450 applications a day. We have already hired many translators.

• Now that the corrupt and repressive Sadaam regime has been ousted, can public- and private-sector employees expect to receive a greater share of their country's vast national wealth in return for their labor?
Answer: That's a tough question. I cannot tell you the answer to it.

• When will Iraqi public money that is being held in trust and monies that have been frozen in overseas foreign bank accounts be made available as investment capital in Iraq?
Answer: I don't know. I have no knowledge of that. Maybe you could learn more about that at the CMCC meetings.

• Who is now and will be controlling Iraqi oil and allocating the profits from Iraqi oil until an Iraqi government is set up?

Answer: Currently the Ministry of Oil is doing that function. We have set up a task force that we're working with to get the ministry up and running. I don't know how profits will be allocated.

Medical: Public Health is in crisis because of shortages of material and human resources, security issues, shortages of medicines and supplies, damage to and looting of facilities, a high number of war-related injuries and illnesses, lack of salaries, inadequate diets, and no access to potable water. So:

• As the interim government of Iraq, what steps has the U.S. taken to address this crisis?

Answer: Our public health team is doing an assessment right now. The Organization for Reconstruction and Humanitarian Assistance (ORHA) [the military's civilian wing] together with the NGOs will provide what is needed.

• When can Iraqis expect their health care system to return to prewar levels of services?

Answer: It's hard to say. I can't provide you with an accurate date.

• To whom can Iraqis address their healthcare needs?

Answer: They can go to the hospitals and health clinics that are open.

Education: All elementary, secondary and post-secondary schools remain closed. Some have been severely damaged and others are currently occupied by U.S. military personal. So:

• What steps have already been taken towards reopening the schools?

Answer: There is an on-going assessment of the condition of the schools and the availability of teachers. Some clean-up has already begun.

• Can Iraqis expect classes in their schools and universities to resume in order to get credit this term? If not, when?

Answer: Whether or not schools reopen depends on the amount of damage to the schools and whether or not the teachers can be found.

• Who will pay the teachers' and professors' salaries?
Answer: I can't answer that question.

• Will there be changes in the curriculum at Iraqi schools? Will it be Iraqis who determine the curriculum of Iraqi children?
Answer: It would have to be Iraqis who determine changes. I cannot predict the sort of changes that Iraqis might choose to make.

Freedom of speech and democracy: The vast majority of Iraqis agree that the previous regime was very undemocratic and used extreme measures to suppress freedom of speech. Iraqis are paying a high price for regaining their freedom of speech and the overthrow of a brutal regime. Iraqis paid dearly in terms of high numbers of civilian casualties, the destruction of property, the loss of social and financial security and in terms of the indefinite suspension of other basic human rights: the right to reasonable healthcare, education, food, shelter, work, income, etc. So:

• Taking into account the above, what mechanisms have been put into place to ensure that Iraqis' newly acquired freedom of speech is accompanied by real democracy and real input into the present and on-going decision-making? – i.e., U.S. government decision-making?
Answer: We brought Iraqis who, with our people, will work together to get the country up and running again and will work to overcome shortcomings and make improvements toward a more democratic society.

• How does the current U.S. interim government identify and

incorporate the emerging leadership of popular religious, social and political organizations?

Answer: I'm not sure what the process is. Check with ORHA.

• Given that many Iraqis (and Arabs in general) have come to see Arabic secular governments as autocracies–their own previous government, for example, or those of Saudi Arabia, Egypt and Iran under the Shah–will the U.S. government be prepared to accept a religious theocracy in Iraq in the event that such leaders are the ones whom the majority of Iraqis wish to elect to govern them?

Answer: I don't know.

• For those Iraqis who need assurance that the current (U.S.) regime is more democratic and more willing to give a real voice to the Iraqi people than the previous regime, what examples would you cite?

Answer: I don't know.

• Insofar as it is Iraqi national wealth and Iraqi oil revenues that will pay for the reconstruction of Iraq, can Iraqis safely assume that it will be Iraqis and not someone else, who determines which firms get the lucrative reconstruction contracts?

Answer: I don't know. Check with ORHA.

• What is the maximum length of time that Iraqis will have to wait before they are permitted self-determination and self-governance?

Answer: I don't know. Check with ORHA.

With so many questions unanswered, Stuart Vriesinga updated the entire list and was able on Thursday, May 1, to submit it to a major who has been conducting the ORHA meetings. This mid-level officer in the occupation's chain of command–to whom CPT now has access–promised replies by Thursday, May 8.

[Ed: In fact those questions were never answered.]

20

Waiting for Garner

Baghdad, Iraq, May 20, 2003

After the fall of Baghdad, the orgy of part-angry, part-gleeful smashing and looting by uncontrollable and uncountable Iraqis that immediately followed was the most visible reaction to the city having just been "liberated." However, other thousands of orderly though equally aggrieved and frustrated Iraqis began to react quite differently.

Although they too have taken to the streets, they are doing it in an orderly fashion. Using one of the occupation's tendered benefits – freedom of speech and assembly – they are hopefully exercising this theoretical new right by heading for the seat of occupation power in order to demonstrate their concerns and wishes and to protest the slow pace with which they are being addressed.

Even as the looters were doing their worst, these other more orderly Iraqis were doing their best to make use of this – for them – novel perquisite of a democratic environment: to vocalize their frustration not just with the perilous and frightening undemocratic incidents from their difficult and too often uncertain totalitarian past, but also to voice their anxieties and anger over the uncertainties of their still undemocratic present – i.e., occupation rule. This occupation has created problems for the still-tormented, long-suffering Iraqi people, and that is what the protesters are trying to convey by means of these demonstrations. The signs and banners they carry proclaim their specific conceptual yearnings or perceived complaints.

Here's a sampling:

"Down with Sadaam. Down with all new repressive policies."

"There will be no roles for criminals in the army."

"Iraq is the home of free people civilizations."

"Liberty, Justice and Independence."

"Shia and Sunna and all nations all united" signed, "SCIRI: Supreme Council of the Islamic Revolution in Iraq."

"Free our high school from U.S. Occupation."

"Where human rights? We need safe residence."

"Mr. Gorner [sic]. We would like your face [sic]." Near to that sign this one: "We ask...Help us."

"Please remove the old aggrissive [sic] administration from Daura oil refinery" signed, "The employees of Daura Refinary [sic]."

And finally this one: "Bush said: Day by day Iraqi people come closely from freedom. We say: Day by day Iraqi people become closely from Hell."

Such protests and language are significant evidence that many Iraqis feel the Allies' wartime propagandizing led them to believe they could expect much more from the occupation than they have been accorded so far. This is why every day a few hundred or a few thousand Iraqis take to the streets to wave placards, written in both Arabic and English, unfurl banners on which their current grievances are displayed, as well as chant or yell their complaints—augmented sometimes by a bullhorn or two—or simply stand together in what seems to be bewildered or confused silence while hoping to be able to share their troubles with any non-Iraqi passerby who will stop long enough to hear them out.

Most often those foreign listeners will be members of the international press or NGO or IO toilers whose mission, in part, is to know and communicate Iraqi needs along with a sense of their exasperation and impatience with the pace of the occupation's restoration of such vital institutions as:

Security: three kinds – 1) law and order capable of protecting businesses, social and governmental institutions and also homes from looting, robbery, or an increasing squatter problem; 2) steady employment paying decent wages that will not go to functionaries of the old regime; and 3) the detention, they claim, from time to time by the occupation of their leaders or would be leaders;

Electrical power to get and keep vital social, commercial and governmental institutions up and running;

Gasoline in plentiful enough supply to enable Iraqis to travel for business or recreation without having to wait in traffic-snarling lines for interminable hours and where, as spring progresses, they are getting more exasperatingly hot each day;

Sewers that work and garbage and trash collection that will preclude citizens who live and work on side streets from falling victim to health problems exacerbated by rising mounds of refuse.

But the main concern for most Iraqis, especially protesters (disappointed as they are with the pace and the vexing aspects of regime-change listed above) is that despite their efforts to be heard, they believe they are not. This explains why at some point during our conversations with many, I am invariably and plaintively asked, "What will you do with what I tell you? What will you do with what you see here?" i.e., their placards and banners. "And whom will you tell about us?"

Whether or not these protests register constructively with those in the occupation who not only are able to respond but – more important than that – who also have the power to respond, is difficult to determine. Decades ago Americans used to chuckle knowingly over a popular cliché that despite its banality still speaks directly – perhaps facetiously – to the problems Iraqis are expressing in the streets. "Let's run it up the flagpole and see who salutes."

Is anyone at the highest level of the occupation saluting – if only to acknowledge that the protesters' concerns are being heard?

Even when it is true that listening is going on behind occupation barriers, that's not the perception of Iraqis outside who are anxiously clutching those placards and banners. One day as we were being herded back from a barbed-wire perimeter outside the entrance to the occupation's main base of operations for the third time by toughly intentional U.S. troopers, one frustrated demonstrator asked, "What is use of speech freedom, if we cannot know that someone is listening?"

"I know what you mean," I answered, "Bush didn't listen to me either."

Another Iraqi in the crowd complained, "Why doesn't Garner talk to us? When we come here, it is like our words are stones dropping in the well. We do not hear them enter the water."

Garner, of course, is retired Lieutenant General Jay Garner who heads up the Pentagon's Office of Rehabilitation and Humanitarian Assistance. I stress "Pentagon," because it is the U.S. military that is running the country right now, and it is the occupation that will still be controlling events on the ground here—through Garner—after an interim puppet government of Iraqis is set up. That event, Garner told a small gathering of NGOs and IOs recently, will happen—he hopes—at the end of this month.

"Puppet government," of course, is my term for what we can expect, not his. To better comprehend the concept: 1) think Afghanistan or, going even further back in time, think Vietnam and the series of puppet governments installed there by the U.S. during that violent humanitarian catastrophe for both Vietnamese and American families and then 2) hope that much better will be accomplished for the sake of the long-suffering Iraqi people with respect to their regime change, which, of course, also was achieved violently.

When it comes to the occupation responses to the concerns expressed by Baghdad citizens in the streets, non-Iraqis find it easier to gauge the occupation's unspoken point of view than Iraqis seem able to do, although even for the internationals it sometimes takes a bit of reading-between-the-lines. Comprehension often dawns as a result of operational assertions about these issues that are uttered by a variety of middle-rank officers who can be accessed fairly easily by internationals but not by most Iraqis. However, these officers are not policymakers but rather the "ours-is-not-to-reason-why" military officials; their job is to carry out policy set by those higher up the chain of command. The basic message not being delivered directly to the people in the streets is that they are expecting too much, too soon.

So what we have here, recalling the cynical words of the sheriff in "Cool Hand Luke," in addition to big-time plea copping, is "a failure to communicate" directly, effectively and efficiently. "You have," said a frequently patronizing and rationalizing mid-level occupation minion (a major assigned to facilitate NGO and IO efforts to deal with the consequences of the humanitarian mess the military created) "to understand that dealing with humanitarian complaints is your work. We're here to facilitate, but you need to do it." (Why is it that every time someone begins an explanation with "You have to understand..." I am inclined to do exactly the opposite?)

Translation of the major's polemic: If things are going too slow to suit the Iraqis, it's the fault of the NGOs and IOs who, because they are in a constant struggle to maintain their independence from the military, are not inclined to salute reflexively whatever and whenever some new assertion – or directive, for that matter – is run up the occupation flagpole.

Meanwhile Iraqi protesters waiting more or less helplessly in streets outside well-protected occupation venues are not getting answers to questions and issues they want addressed. Instead they are met with the impassive scrutiny of soldiers guarding Allied perimeters or their oft-repeated commands to "move back" whenever it is feared a crowd may be on the verge of getting out of control. So the demonstrations continue to reflect a pervasive feeling of being "had" by the occupation. This was expressed the other day by a remarkably good-natured Iraqi university graduate waving a placard demanding the occupation stop giving jobs to former

Baath Party regulars and instead give one to him. "Mister," he said, "do you know 'Waiting for Godot'?"

"You mean the play about the two men who don't move but talk and talk and talk while waiting for Mr. Godot – but he never comes?

"Yes, yes that one."

"So?"

"I think Godot is God. You think so, too?"

"Yes, I think that is who the author meant."

"So, Mister?"

"What?"

"Where is Jay Garner?"

21

Will the Real Ali Baba Please Stand up?

Amman, Jordan, May 19, 2003

Not far from the east bank of the Tigris River in downtown Baghdad a massive sculpted monument to one of the most famous stories of the *Arabian Nights* – Ali Baba and the 40 Thieves – stands in the middle of a large and busy traffic roundabout. Installed by the Sadaam regime, it's a spectacular work marking the moment in the story when Ali Baba's loyal slave girl, having discovered the plot to kill her oblivious master, pours oil into the 37 jars in which the larcenous thieves have been stealthily hiding while awaiting a signal from their chief to burst forth, kill Ali Baba and then recover their ill-gotten loot. This particular story chosen from the saga of a thousand and one tales must resonate deeply in the Iraq psyche for it to be portrayed in this conspicuous manner. And more than one Iraqi to whom I've talked has referred to their deposed and still-missing former leader as "Sadaam: Ali Baba."

A retired scientist expanded further on the metaphor saying, "All Iraq is a septic tank and Sadaam was the cover. I think he was Ali Baba." This man is no post-Sadaam, knee-jerk occupation supporter. He lives a block away from the university campus where he worked for decades. "Rumsfeld bombed it," he complained. "He destroyed many buildings and I cried when I saw this. Rumsfeld is Ali Baba."

Another university official said quite angrily, "I did not agree always with Sadaam, but he made Iraq a very great country for us. We were the most advanced for all the people of the Middle East. But Bush!? I think he was bigger Ali Baba. He made us poor again. Nothing here is great now."

Bush and Sadaam, however, are only the tip of the Ali Baba iceberg. The label applies to a multitude of other relationships. A Christian cab driver, in discussing the Ayatollah Khomeini, the Taliban and the situation in the Sudan, showed his own anxieties when he said, "Maybe Muslims will be Ali Baba." He worries, he says, "because there are too many of them. I don't think they will protect us like Sadaam. But, what can we do? Tariq Aziz (a Christian) was Ali Baba too."

From the beginning of the war, many of the most influential Muslims, especially Shia clergy, have kept the "Ali Baba" imagery at arm's length. Thus Jay Garner, the elusive, outgoing Pentagon choice to preside over the Allies' now-creaking-behind-schedule nation-building process was branded an "Ali Baba" even before he stepped back on conquered Iraqi soil; his Shia critics were that certain about their prophecies of inevitable occupation ineptness and worse. Garner remains a terrible reminder of their catastrophic legacy from the Gulf War when he became a hero to the Kurds in the north whom the U.S. protected from Sadaam, while Iraq's Shia, after being encouraged by the first President Bush to revolt, were abruptly deserted by the U.S. and left to twist slowly, slowly in Sadaam's decimating wind.

The "Ali Baba" label was also applied early on to exiled occupation favorites who were allowed to return with the Allies—the most prominent being Ahmad Chalabi, a convicted embezzler wanted in two Arab nations—Jordan and Lebanon. Upon reaching Baghdad and seizing some buildings for his headquarters, he formed a militia that is being gratuitously armed by the U.S. In fact, any Iraqi linked to an appointed interim civil entity is automatically an "Ali Baba," so we hear "Ali Baba" rumblings connected to the names of all the presumably occupation-vetted candidates involved in Mosul's imminent "city council" elections.

Those profiteering from the petrol black market are being derisively and angrily labeled "Ali Babas" as are the Iraqis who try to take cuts in the long, long lineups for gas at legitimate filling stations. With the petrol crisis, the occupation can't win for losing. In order to alleviate shortages and undercut black-marketeers, they let it be known, but not very loudly or efficiently, they were setting up distribution stations where eight gallons would be given free to each customer. "But," as one cab driver said to me, "where are these places? I cannot find them. I think it is an Ali Baba trick."

The thousands of squatters who have been moving into bombed-out ministries or taking over empty homes are the latest Ali Baba manifestation, as are the still inextinguishable and apparently irrepressible looters. However, there is considerable agreement among Iraqis that the most consequential Ali Baba-style looting in the aggregate is being conducted by the occupation. Why else, we are continually reminded, would Allied soldiers have been sent to guard only the Oil Ministry during the first days following the fall of Baghdad.

There's a dimension to this Ali Baba-labeling phenomenon that is curious. The name Ali Baba which has become synonymous in Baghdad with thievery and chicanery, is nevertheless somewhat a misnomer. After all, in the story Ali Baba was a poor man who serendipitously became rich by seizing an opportunity to steal from bloodthirsty thieves what wasn't theirs in the first place. His most notable traits were an incredible naïveté and a myopic obliviousness to imminent danger. In some ways he was a prototype Beverly Hillbilly or maybe Inspector Clouseau. Despite a chain of violent tragedies, mayhem and potential tragedies swirling about him, because of events he had unknowingly set in motion, he nevertheless escapes without a scratch. Even though he wasn't the villain in the piece, nor by any yardstick the craftiest, his name these days has become synonymous with thievery and trickery.

Strange.

But perhaps not so strange. Ali Baba was poor, but he wasn't entirely honest. First, even though what he found were ill-gotten gains, he nevertheless did take what wasn't his. And second, restitution never seemed to occur to him, an attitude somewhat similar to the Allied troops' zealously guarding the Iraqi Oil Ministry while letting other critical venues be looted and burned. And there was also the apparent paucity of foresight and planning (or was it more sinister than that?) that resulted in an absolute dearth of Allied military police trained to do what regular troops have no professional competence to do – protect property and enforce order until professional and trustworthy civilian competence can be reëstablished,

Besides this, there was a glaring absence of any professional force for infrastructural resuscitation and construction. Such a group should have been poised in the desert to move in immediately behind the occupying Allied army. Apparently our myopic U.S. administration was oblivious to (or perhaps determined to ignore) the cascade of warnings beamed from almost everywhere as to the inevitable consequences of doggedly conducting regime change on the cheap, because no such follow-up contingent was provided.

Thinking through all this, I realize the folks in Baghdad have got it right after all. In Iraq there are more than enough Ali Babas these days – foreign and domestic – to go around.

22

These Things Take Time

Birmingham, Alabama, June 7, 2003

Professionals adept at waging war and promoting the idea that war is an appropriate means for establishing peace can be counted on usually to promise that peace will follow in war's wake. Once again in Iraq these folk are proving how woefully incompetent they are when it comes to waging the peace – which they insist will follow. Street protests and worse continue: tangible demonstrations of Iraqi exasperation and impatience with the pace of the occupation's restoration of such vital institutions as security, education, power, fuel, sanitation and health.

To survive a community needs security, the presence of law and order capable of protecting businesses, social and governmental institutions and individuals and their homes from looting, robbery or expropriation by squatters. One indelible image I have of postwar Iraq is the sidewalks of Baghdad eerily emptied of the presence of women. They have been staying warily at home. It's almost as if "Left Behind" suddenly came true in Baghdad and the only humans left are men, youths and boys.

While my wife Sis and I were in Baghdad, we only saw one military police vehicle in the streets. Maintaining order and security is still being carried out mainly by the occupiers' professional fighters – not by the military's professional police specialists whose usual job is to establish and maintain social order and security in occupied lands until indigenous replacements can be organized and trained. Instead, the men and women who fought their way across Iraq, who are not professional where policing is concerned, are the ones who are entrusted with policing the country and training the new local police forces as well. But that's like expecting a National Football League quarterback to train a Major League baseball pitcher to throw fastballs and then do the pitching until the replacement gets up to speed.

To me this is an unconscionable strategy. When I first contemplated this ploy, I used the word "blunder" instead of "strategy," then I realized the situation is so obviously and basically wrong, that it can't have been a blunder. It had to be a predetermined strategy. But why? Perhaps it has something to do with what President Bush crowed to cheering troops in Qatar recently: "Mission accomplished," he told them.

What mission? If the current instability that our military uses to justify putting off getting to the promised interim stage of shared governance was the mission, then I guess he's right. The mission of putting and keeping the U.S. in charge of Iraq's future has indeed been accomplished and despite earlier assurances, that does not seem likely to change any time soon. Unfortunately the mission of providing employment has not been accomplished. Instead of awarding positions for expediency to murderous or murder-acquiescing functionaries of the old regime, our representatives should be organizing jobs that pay a living wage for the massive numbers left without work.

There is also the issue – protesters claim – of why the occupation officials continue to detain current leaders or would-be leaders and some of their followers under questionable conditions. A Christian Peacemaking Team colleague recently reported seeing a U.S. military truck moving down a Baghdad street carrying in the back a number of blindfolded men. The last time I saw a chilling scene like that was in Palestine's West Bank.

So much of the country's infrastructure is being ignored. School supplies and equipment, looted and destroyed during the war, have not been replaced. Girls' schools as well as some boys' schools are staying closed because their students are afraid to leave home to face the escalating peril in the streets. There is no electrical power to get vital social, commercial and governmental institutions up and running. It seems incredible that in a country with one of the world's largest oil reserves, gasoline is not in plentiful enough supply to enable Iraqis to travel for business or recreation without having to wait in traffic-snarling lines for interminable hours. Even cooking gas is in short supply.

And so the list of problems goes on. Power-dependent water purification facilities and sewage disposal systems that work are needed as well as garbage and trash collections throughout the city to prevent diseases being exacerbated by mounds of refuse. A viable functioning health and nutrition infrastructure is absent and hospitals are still being looted of medicine and equipment while adequate food supplies remain out of reach of the city's poor.

Most Iraqis, especially the protesters frustrated by the distressing effects so far of regime change, feel that despite their efforts to be heard, they are not listened to. Even more distressing to them is the occupation's insistence that Iraqis are being unrealistic in their expectations. More than one of our occupation official has said to me, "These things take time." The truth is that before the invasion of Iraq, planning and preparations to deal with such "things" apparently was minimal. Despite warnings from professionals experienced in dealing with such situations, neither matériel nor specialists were positioned in the desert—to the rear of our conquering troops—ready to be moved in promptly after Baghdad, Basra and other cities fell.

Why? As one civilian rehabilitation consultant attached to the occupation told me, "We're waiting for the Bechtel man." Anyone not familiar with Bechtel? That's the huge West Coast industrial conglomerate to which the administration gave most of the lucrative rehabilitation and rebuilding contracts without taking any competitive bids. The "Bechtel man" exemplifies the lucrative privatization of the rebuilding phase of the occupation. He is not about to get things going until the security situation has stabilized.

In one of the commentaries sent back from Baghdad, I ascribed the occupation posture to the example set by its local head, Jay Garner, a retired general appointed by our "defense" department. Two days later he was fired. There was some hope his replacement, L. Paul Bremer, formerly from the state department, was a sign Washington was reacting constructively to the complaints they had been hearing about the slow pace of reviving the most vital elements of Iraq's institutional and technological infrastructure. It seems clear now Washington was reacting not to the complaints, but only to the obvious fact that the natives were restless.

The result of regime change number two in Iraq, i.e., axing General Garner (regime change number one, of course, was axing Saddam Hussein) has been the breaking of assurances that interim power-sharing between the military and hand-picked Iraqis would begin by the end of May. Instead that significant "liberation" event has been postponed and the Iraqis, feeling increasingly patronized and double crossed, are more restless than ever. Meanwhile, in spite of President Bush's "mission accomplished" pronouncement, the body count of U.S. soldiers is inching up day after day

The Iraqis continue to suffer serious material, social and political deprivations at the hands of the open-ended military rule that has been a front for Washington's neo-carpet bagging reconstruction policy—which is being masqueraded as "nation building." I not only worry about Iraqis caught in the escalating violence, but also about the many conscience-stricken young GIs we met in Baghdad who are in daily danger of being picked off, one-by-one and two-by-two by the large number of Iraqis disillusioned by an occupation they had been led to believe would be liberating. We may soon have to face the fact that the number of post-Bush "mission accomplished" deaths among Allied soldiers will eclipse the number of those who died during the invasion. Don't expect many of those left by the end of 2003 to be home for Christmas.

23

While You Were Gone

Hebron, West Bank, Palestine, July 5, 2003

Every time my wife and I leave Palestine and Israel and head for home – when our visas are about to run out – we hope things won't get worse here while we are back in the States; but sadly we know they will.

And, sure enough, they do.

Similarly, when we come back from the U.S. after traveling to cities and towns talking and writing about the seriously deteriorating security situation in Palestine, we hope that things won't get worse once we get back to the territories; but sadly we know they will.

And they do.

Trying to characterize what happened here this past winter and spring, a Palestinian friend said, "While you were gone, this was a time of sadness."

We were surprised that she could term the situation in such a relatively mild fashion. That's because despite "road map" calls for ending provocative settlement and other confiscatory activities in the West Bank, which might – just might – discourage violent Palestinian reprisals, there has been a glut of discouraging events. These suggest there has actually been an acceleration of the Israeli decades-long, coercive campaign to convince Arab residents – Muslim and Christian – that Palestine is no longer a safe or welcome place for them to live. While we were gone, Palestinian patience, as always, had been sorely tried.

In a tiny but typical portion of the West Bank – Hebron's Old City – I experienced this frustration firsthand. After we left Palestine last January, the Israeli army extended its control over H2 by appropriating a piece of H1. This not-so-surprising absorption stifled a once-vital H1 commercial neighborhood of hard-pressed Palestinian small shop proprietors and street vendors whose businesses had the misfortune of lying a few hundred yards away from the de jure dividing line between the two zones.

H2, the area of Hebron consigned to Israel after the post-Oslo Wye River Accords, includes an enclave of small settlements whose militant Orthodox Jewish residents, backed by the Israeli army, over the years have been stunningly successful at squelching and closing down most Palestinian business inside the Old City. Such pressure drove more than three-quarters of the population to move away. H1 is the area of Hebron granted to the Palestinian National Authority but it was totally reoccupied by Israel last summer. The perimeter of the extended H2 engulfs the now mostly moribund Hebron marketplace known as Bab iZaweyya.

The Israeli army blocked access to this once boisterous, lively, exhilarating market by setting down huge cement block barricades in the streets feeding to it. Until then, Bab iZaweyya had been the scene of tightly packed throngs of chattering, slow-moving shoppers on foot who overflowed into the even more crowded streets. Stuffed full of gridlocked taxis, jitneys and private cars, the streets were also lined with long rows of produce and small goods stands, not to mention parked cars and pedestrians. The drivers, confronting those animate and inanimate encroachers on the street, were notable for their collective impatient contribution to an already considerable din because of their reflexive efforts to honk, yell, holler or scream their way through the throttled intersection at the heart of Bab iZaweyya.

No one was surprised by this latest landgrab. The Israeli army had been insinuating its intentions for several weeks late last year. During the busiest part of the day, tanks would suddenly come tearing into the intersection, crushing or upsetting the portable stands, scattering goods and shoppers as they went. They would knock over and chase off not just those in the streets, but those on sidewalks too. At other times squads of Israeli soldiers would dash into the area, arbitrarily declaring curfew, gruffly shouting at shoppers to leave and ordering all businesses to shut down.

These disruptions went on for several weeks until one morning, shortly after the first of the year, the barricades suddenly appeared. Now, except for a few stands still operating on the sidewalks, the area is relatively subdued, very calm and much quieter than before. The only traffic through it consists of people mostly on their way somewhere else. Businesses and the consumer traffic they attract are moving uptown further and further away from H2 and its handful of demanding Orthodox Jewish settlers. The two or three blocks between the former boundary of the two zones, marked by the Beit Romano checkpoint at one end and Bab iZaweyya at the other, are distinguished by a dwindling number of shops that are still open. Of the 100 shops I counted last week, 60 were closed.

As hard hit as that stretch has been, the shops lining the principal market street inside H2's Old City have suffered far worse because consumers are less and less inclined to venture down there to shop because of the continuing settler-motivated Israeli military and police harassment and enforced closures. The inevitable result will be that more Old City proprietors can be expected to give up and close down in the months ahead. Currently, of the nearly 100 shops lining the streets between the CPT apartment in the Old City and the Beit Romano checkpoint, only ten are still operating. Six months ago three times that number were open for business.

"Why do I stay open?" one shopkeeper friend reflected rhetorically. "What else is there to do?" he finally answered.

But then he declared, "I will not leave."

Meanwhile, at the other end of the Old City in the very center of H2, the border police have severely restricted foot traffic through the special security zone surrounding the Ibrahimi Mosque. Now Palestinians who want to pass through the western half of the zone to the eastern half can't because to do that they must cross Shuhada Street, which cuts through it. These tightened access rules apply for the first time to CPT as well. We are also subject to more frequent ID checks than ever before, even by soldiers and border police who know us by sight. In the past our CPT identification cards would suffice to answer such challenges. Now only our passports will do.

A major stretch of Shuhada Street had long been closed to Palestinians because of the part that runs downhill from Tel Rumeida, the small Israeli settlement at the western edge of H2, eastward to the special security zone a few yards from the Ibrahimi Mosque. Now the rest of Shuhada Street that runs northward from the mosque through the special security zone has been ruled off-limits to us, too, so what should be an easy five-minute walk across the zone is instead a frustrating 30-plus minute, steep detour around the mosque. If one doesn't want to walk, getting from one side of the zone to the other requires a 20-minute cab ride clear around Hebron.

"The cost can add up," I mentioned to a Palestinian acquaintance.

"We don't count the cost," she said. "We count the time."

Another friend mentioned offhandedly, "If we apply, we can get a permit to walk through."

"Has anyone got one yet?"

"No one will even try," he said proudly and passionately. "What Palestinian would ever ask for a permit to walk on their own street to their own home?"

24

Catch-22s in the Land of Milk and Honey

Hebron, West Bank, Palestine, July 28, 2003

Al No'man is a Palestinian village situated across a wadi and up a high hill to the north of Beit Sahour, a legendary-historic location (take your choice) of the fields where shepherds, so the carol goes, "lay watching their sheep." To the east lies the huge, illegal Israeli settlement (according to international standards) of Har Homa. This blot on the landscape, which has been shrewdly built by Israel on the leveled site of a once beautiful forested Palestinian hilltop, is blocking expansion of the burgeoning metropolitan Bethlehem area to the south of it. Other smaller settlements that ring Bethlehem to the east, south and west are effecting an encirclement that is choking off future growth of this regional center of Palestinian life.

As with so many of the larger settlements in the West Bank, Har Homa has the appearance of an updated medieval fortress town – an obscene, in-your-face fortification whose privileged citizens hunker down behind thick walls intended to shield them from any outburst of anger from the displaced, serf-like Palestinians living outside and beneath its walls. These unfortunates continue to be excluded systematically from sharing the benefits of the contemporary feudal lifestyle imposed on them by Israel's nouveau nobles with their cruel Crusader-like chivalry. Palestine clearly is not for the Palestinians but for the Israelis.

Tall construction cranes towering above Har Homa rooftops testify to the additional fact that the "road map" is not a consideration in Palestine. Settlement expansion continues. In addition, the "separation fence," also known as the "wall of hate," is still snaking its way through the West Bank, effectively annexing into Israel tens of thousands of *dunams* of farmland as it goes, removing them unilaterally from any future negotiations that may be launched to determine the borders of a Palestinian State.

The Green Line demarcating the borders of Israel/Palestine at the end of the 1967 war long ago was transmuted by the Israeli press and government spokespersons into something called the Seam Line, which these days is being turned into an Invisible Line outlining nothing. The line is relentlessly being superseded by Israel's greedy dash into a modern-day Cherokee Strip (here called the West Bank) in order to grab off the fertile Palestinian land and its water lying between the Green/Seam/Invisible Line and the series of villages, towns or cities in which Palestinians live. Clearly the wall is intended to be the new Green Line and as a result of its snaky path, it is swallowing up considerable Palestinian territory. The West Bank, when viewed from above, resembles Swiss cheese much more than it does a sovereign state with territorial integrity.

The wall is one more example of the skewed tabletop on which the "road map" was cynically conceived. The onus has been on the Palestinians to accomplish much more than Israelis. This kind of provocation reflects enormous Israeli chutzpa constituting an outrageous occupational dare, a cynical prodding of the collective Palestinian patience. Stretched to the breaking point, utterly aggrieved individuals might well resort to violent and inevitably unproductive responses against the provocateurs. It is in this terrible sea of troubles that millions of Palestinians are desperately treading. If the current cease-fire breaks down, Israel, of course, will have another excuse, another alibi (which presumably would be endorsed by an ever-compliant Washington) for calling the whole thing off and resuming an even more relentless full-steam-ahead campaign of territorial thievery and appalling humiliations.

Consider the village of Al No'man. When one stands on the hilltop overlooking the wadi lying between it and Beit Sahour, one can clearly observe the path of the latest section of the hate wall being relentlessly nudged from east to west around the village toward Har Homa. The residents of Al No'man have no power to protect themselves from the consequences of having this wall constructed between them and the rest of the West Bank. They are in a unique situation because some time ago the village was annexed into Jerusalem, which lies just to the north, but the residents all have West Bank IDs; this means they are not Israeli citizens, even though soon they will be cut off from Palestine and the West Bank by the wall.

Since West Bankers are not allowed to live in Israel, in effect Al No'man's residents are squatters on their own land. Meanwhile their children aren't permitted to attend nearby schools in Jerusalem because they're not Israeli, so they go to school in not-so-nearby Beit Sahour. The wall eventually will cut them off from Beit Sahour, but so far this result – plus many others – of this Catch-22 has not been resolved. Its citizens continue to suffer the usual occupation indignities: home demolitions, settler harassment, no permission to build on their own land while they see Israeli homes shooting up all around them in the steadily encroaching settlements, destruction of crops and water pipes, uprooting of telephone poles, the tearing up of their roads and also the barricades set up blocking access in and out of the village.

Meanwhile several kilometers to the south in the Ba'qaa Valley, bordered to the west by Hebron and more ominously by the Israeli settlements of Harsina and Kiryat Arba, farmers are caught in another Catch-22 vice. This summer Israeli settlers from both colonies have been busily ratcheting up their campaign of carving new roads or extending old ones down from their settlements into and through Palestinian farmland. By means of threats and wire fences that have been installed to divide up the fields, armed settler security guards have forbidden Palestinians from entering those fields to tend to their own crops – mainly grapes. When the farmers complain to the Israeli army, they are told that the settlers have no right to do that, but then when the Palestinians try to enter their vineyards and a confrontation with armed settler security guards looms, the soldiers stop the Palestinians "in order to protect them from the settlers."

Barred by the soldiers, the farmers then complain to the "civil administration," the army bureaucracy that runs the West Bank ("civil administration" is a semantic obfuscation designed to cover up the fact that the Israeli army controls and runs every aspect of life in the occupied territories. When it serves its purpose, it has the power to overrule the Israeli courts in the name of security). The civil administration will agree with the farmers that the settlers are out of order, but then tells them it is the soldiers' job to keep the settlers in line.

So this decades-long dirty war continues – the dirty war the United States has helped Israel wage against the Palestinians and their land to an excess beyond all humane logic and justification.

"The Israelis are playing cat-and-mouse with us" a Palestinian activist complained to me last week.

"The game could go on for a long time, couldn't it?" I asked.

"Not so long," my friend answered. "Time is running out for us, especially the farmers. We are in what you call a Catch-22. You see, the settlers use their guns to frighten the farmers from their grapes. Then the soldiers say that we have the right to be there, but the soldiers won't let us go past the settlers, so we don't save the grapes. And the civil administration does nothing."

"And?"

"Well, there is an Israeli rule. It says that if we don't work our land for two or three years it can be confiscated."

"Catch-22?"

"Yes, the Catch-22."

25

The Baladyeh and the Baptismal Font
Part 1

Bethlehem, West Bank, Palestine, August 11, 2003

Tuqu' is a Palestinian village way off the beaten tourist track. My friends Hisham Ali and George Rishmawi had taken me there to prove that it should be included.

"It is not enough," Hisham asserted, "for tourists to come to Bethlehem and go to souvenir shops and the Church of the Nativity and think they have seen Palestine. Maybe three times as many people live in the countryside and villages, but due to the occupation, village life is one of the most threatened cultures in Palestine."

Then George reminded me that before 1948 there had been 920 Palestinian villages in what became Israel. Now because of the Israelis' campaign of systematic destruction and depopulation there are only 430 villages still lived in by Palestinians. The menace of being forced out is facing villagers in the West Bank, and it is becoming more perilous every day. It is an especially critical time for Palestinian villagers living within the shadow of the ever-expanding Israeli settlements – none of which existed before 1967.

Tuqu', on the other hand, boasts one of the longest histories of continuous community life in the region. "When you come here, you can see the actual signs of life from prehistoric ages all the way to now," said Hisham.

Ancient Tuqu', often spelled Tekoah, Tekoa or Teqoa in English-language Bibles, is overlooked, but it is a fascinating historical site-to-be-seen. One reason is that spelling it Tuqu' on contemporary English language maps does not convey any historic relevance. Somehow the voracious Palestinian-property-swallowing, heritage-filching, nouveau Israeli settlement of Teqoa does. In fact, before 1967, Israeli Teqoa was just another uninhabited Palestinian hilltop overlooking vast Palestinian lands that had been in continuous use for aeons by semi-nomads and farmers from Tuqu' and other villages in the Judean hills southeast of Bethlehem. It was a common, pastoral and agrarian expanse which stretched all the way to the Dead Sea, 15 miles to the east. Tuqu' had been a lively population center for most of human history, while Israeli Tekoa just across a wadi from Tuqu' had been a place where sheep (and goats and camels) could safely graze.

Not any more.

The lands east of Tuqu', for centuries the permissible domain of Palestinian shepherds and farmers, are now off-limits to them but decidedly on-limits for Israeli settlers in Teqoa and their expanding nearby sister settlements. Since the Oslo Accords most of the vast grazing and agricultural areas have been barred to Palestinians, so while there is room for the settlements to grow, there is none for Tuqu'. Therefore, for most of the year, there is no work for its residents.

Having lost their pastoral and agricultural livelihoods, they have been turned into mostly idle day-laborers in Israel's construction industry. Since the uprising began three years ago, they are rarely allowed to cross the Green Line into Israel where the jobs are. "You could call what's going on today, cultural genocide," Hisham claimed, "because our old way of life is almost extinct. Tuqu' and the other villages here were most prosperous at one time. Now they are some of the poorest."

The neglected, unoccupied archeological site of biblical Tekoah merges with contemporary inhabited Tuqu'. At a distance, the old uncared-for site appears to be a large hilltop of jumbled rocks and ancient building stones, but in the company of Palestinians like Hisham Ali and George Rishmawi, who are proudly conversant with the history and archeology of the place, the rocky prominence and its history comes alive quickly.

Here are the still identifiable foundation stones of the Basilica of St. Nicholas – not the Santa Claus St. Nicholas but, explained Hisham, the one "who came here in the year 334 after Christ from Anatolia and established monasteries for monks who wanted to live in the desert. In fact," he went on, "it was a very lively place. There were about 650 monasteries in the area." Nearby are caves, once lived in, which can be entered easily and explored, while all about are pottery shards from premodern times, as well as ancient cisterns and the remains of walls of Byzantine structures too big to be homes. Their scale indicates they were shelters established to deal with the booming early Christian business of religious tourism. Here, too, are remnants of the Crusader, Mamluk and Ottoman periods. The village's Byzantine past was, relatively speaking, only yesterday. Agricultural and pre-pottery artifacts dating from as early as 8,000 B.C. have been found, clearly verifying ancient Tuqu' as one of the earliest and continuous human communities to have sprouted in the region.

One day some 2,750 years ago a shepherd and pruner of fig trees named Amos set out on a walk from his hometown Tekoah, past Jerusalem, the capital of the southern Hebrew kingdom of Judah, and into scriptural and ethical history. He did not stop until he reached Bethel, the capital of the northern Hebrew kingdom of Israel where he persistently and publicly proclaimed that God had told him to warn the Israelites of terrible times ahead because of their failure to "let justice flow like a stream and righteousness like an ever-flowing river."

Byzantine Christians like St. Nicholas and others were among the first to see the inspirational value of Amos' birthplace and, as a result, turned it into a long-running, must-see pilgrimage destination. Early on, a basilica to St. Amos was erected, but unlike the known location of the St. Nicholas Basilica, the whereabouts of St. Amos has not been pinpointed yet. While scripture has nothing to say about the death of Amos, nor his burial place, tradition has it that the Amos Basilica, erected some 1,000 years after his time, was located atop a cave in which his tomb can be found. Of course, there is little hope of ever finding the verifiable tomb of Amos, but the chances of locating a cave on top of which are building stones arranged in a basilica pattern of the Byzantine era remains potentially real.

Despite the potential lure of Tuqu's history, modern-day Israel does not seem interested in calling attention to the significance of the site. "If they had," said Hisham, "they would have made it a tourist place like Herodion a couple of miles from here."

Another reason dawned on me. Modern Israel never has been inclined to focus attention on sites pertaining to the so-called Minor Prophets who, as far as I can judge, were quite major because they spent their days publicly, persistently and courageously railing against their own people's idolatrous abuse of power and wealth, calling attention to the fact that God's promise to them of land had been and remained conditional on their best behavior, and in the opinion of those prophets, that was going from bad to worse.

As we toured the site, we were eyed by three or four lean and hungry looking men who were there before we came and looked as if they would be staying on long after we left. They were treasure hunters from the village looking to boost their mostly nonexistent incomes. To support their children they searched for old coins, pieces of pottery, an old lamp – anything that they could quietly sell to ravenous antiquities dealers.

"Palestinians know this is definitely destructive to our culture and heritage," Hisham said, "but, hey, what can people do? What can a father with kids do? And besides there are no guards to stop them. This place is neglected beyond belief."

"Why not fence it off and install guards?"

"It's not that we don't have the funds, but our hands are not free," George explained. "If the Palestinian Authority wanted to help by doing some work here and fence this place in, do you think the soldiers would allow them to do that?"

That's when, by way of sad and frustrating example, I was told the stories of the theft of ancient Tuqu's most prestigious artifact—a huge baptismal font that graced the Basilica of St. Nicholas for centuries. Its disappearance was traced to sophisticated Israeli interests involved in the plundering of archeological sites—and the ongoing official Israeli pressure to destroy the contemporary villagers' proud, new municipal headquarter building, known as the Baladyeh.

(TO BE CONTINUED)

26

The Baladyeh and the Baptismal Font
Part 2

Bethlehem, West Bank, Palestine, August 25, 2003

The impressive eight-ton, eight-sided, pinkish limestone baptismal font rested for hundred of years amidst the tumbled, scattered, rocky ruins of the biblical and post-biblical site of Tuqu', the West Bank Palestinian village known in English as Tekoa. For a long time it was the only sizable, intact relic remaining from the Byzantine era when Tuqu' had been an important destination for Christian pilgrims making their devout way from shrine to shrine in the Judean hill country southeast of Jerusalem and Bethlehem.

The baptismal font had stood upright down through the centuries in the ancient Basilica of St. Nicholas, while the basilica itself and other neighboring buildings erected to cater to the needs of the pilgrim trade were gradually dismantled. Stone by stone their structural remains were incorporated into Crusader, then Mamluk and finally Ottoman buildings, homes and defensive walls at successor sites only a few yards to the north. The font itself— five-feet high and five-feet across—was shaped from a limestone block extracted from a quarry famous in the Bethlehem area called *Slyeb*, which in English translates as "the small cross."

Slyeb is no longer open for business. In theory, it could be, but not too long ago the quarry was made to disappear – apparently forever – and now lies buried beneath the foundations of the large Israeli West Bank settlement of Gilo. That new settlement is one of the chain of settlements designed and built to encircle the Palestinian towns, Christian and Muslim, which comprise the greater Bethlehem area, thereby limiting their potential for growth.

Ten years ago the contemporary village of Tuqu' was smaller and thus situated further away from the ruins of the basilica than it is now. Then in the early 1990s the West Bank was under an occupational lockdown similar to what is the norm today, so at night when the engines of Israeli army vehicles were heard rumbling about the village or the adjacent archeological site, most villagers moved inside to keep out of potential harm's way. Bitter and often painfully harassing experiences year after year during the long occupation for those who didn't prudently stay indoors had sown the wisdom of such caution.

Late one night sounds of vehicles moving about the unprotected antiquities site south of the village were heard along with other purposeful mechanical whirrings, clankings, clatterings and winchings – all of which were enough to keep people inside wondering what was going on. It was not until the next morning that Tuqu's villagers became aware of the incredible fact that the baptismal font was gone – all eight tons of it!

My friends Hisham Ali and George Rishmawi had brought me to Tuqu' because "the story about what happened next – the search for the baptismal font – is important," Hisham explained. "It is an actual hard-solid account about the Palestinians' pride in their cultural heritage. It is the story about a 100 percent Muslim town chasing a piece of stone that is Christian and that is over 1500 years old."

"Remember," continued George, "the village is also proud that the prophet Amos came from here. He is their heritage too. All that tells you something."

For four years there was little the villagers could do except lament the loss of the only remaining artifact which, because of its size, had dramatically represented so much of their proud cultural heritage and history. As to what actually happened to the baptismal font, there were rumors that had the ring of truth. Most seemed to be focused on shady Israeli interests (antiquities dealers and their well-heeled clients) already involved in the looting and clandestine purchase of artifacts from undeveloped Holy Land archeological sites. Their partners were often Palestinians who knew a certain locale and the treasures still available for plucking. It was also thought that at times the looters were aided – perhaps inadvertently – by the Palestinians' fear of ever-present, hear-no-evil-see-no-evil Israeli army patrols. Their proximity could keep villagers shut up safely and prudently in their homes at night instead of sounding an alarm while the looting took place.

There came some hopeful rumors that the huge artifact was turning out to be very difficult to spirit out of the West Bank. There were whispers that it was hidden not too far away – in the Bethlehem area, but doing something concrete with the information seemed beyond the capability of the village. Then came 1997 and Oslo II and things began to happen that provided the Muslim village the courage to mount a serious campaign to get its Christian artifact back. That year the Palestinian Authority was given administrative control over the villages of the West Bank and Gaza. As a result there was a revolution in the administration of many Palestinian villages, including Tuqu'.

For the first time Palestinian municipalities were created. In Tuqu' and elsewhere management was ceded to traditional tribal elders. Finding themselves not up to the task of planning, initiating and carrying out sorely needed improvements, Tuqu's elders soon relinquished the reins of local power to the village's younger generation. Despite the rigors of the harassing occupation that had stymied the older villagers, the younger leadership was able to make things happen. An energetic mayor, Suleiman Abu Mufarreh, was chosen. Quickly he initiated several projects including building the village's first municipal headquarters building, known in Palestinian cities, towns and villages as the Baladyeh, and launching a campaign to retrieve the baptismal font.

In telling me the story of trying to get back the baptismal font, the mayor first supplied me with some background. "You know, the Israelis did not take care of our shrines," he said, "because, it seems, they were important for the Christians and not for the Israelis. In fact, before the first Oslo agreement in 1993 they dug trenches here for 45 days. When they did not come up with any significant remains—for them—they quit."

The mayor paused and then added, "That same month, the font was stolen." Four years later, installed as mayor, Suleiman decided to retain private investigators who in fairly quick order found there had been more than one attempt to move the font from its hiding places in the West Bank to Israel to complete the sale, but each time, because of the illegality of the scheme, the looters were thwarted. It was now stored with an accomplice across a wadi from Gilo in Beit Jala, who had arranged for it to be hidden there. The investigators found out where. "When we went to the hiding place, the baptismal font was in a field covered with branches," the mayor said, "and the man keeping it told us it had been moved maybe three times but never for very long."

Once found, the Palestinian Authority's Minister of Antiquities ruled the font should belong to the people of Tuqu', so it was brought back home. "But," said the mayor, "I do not think it will be safe at the ruins of St. Nicholas Basilica, so we will put it in front of the Baladyeh in a very small garden that we are planting for it, which is almost ready."

These days it is standing temporarily—it is hoped—behind walls in an orchard adjoining the house of a villager. Whether it can be installed triumphantly in the garden in front of Tuqu's new Baladyeh is uncertain, because as soon as the villagers, with much voluntary sweat and expenditure of personal funds, started putting the building up, attempts—by settlers and the Israeli army to get it torn down—began.

(TO BE CONTINUED)

27

The Baladyeh and the Baptismal Font
Part 3

Bethlehem, West Bank, Palestine, August 26, 2003

Before 1997 and before the Oslo II Accords furnished historic assent to Palestinian administration of West Bank communities, the typical, occupation-beset Palestinian village of Tuqu' – situated in the Judean hills southeast of Bethlehem – had no modern civic institutions of any kind. "We had very urgent needs," said Suleiman Abu Mufarreh, Tuqu's young mayor. "Not just repairing infrastructure, but building it."

"We were a traditional village," he said. "So, at first, twelve elders of the village became the members of the new Palestinian Authority-authorized municipal council. "After six months," he continued, "there were many disagreements. Nothing could get done." So the village elders asked the younger generation to take over and form a council to manage Tuqu's affairs, and Mufarreh was chosen to lead it.

The successor council realized a master plan was needed so it could make informed decisions about such needs as roads, agriculture, medical support, health care, education, schools, sewage, water treatment and public buildings. "Without a master plan there were always problems," the mayor admitted. "But even after we had one, there were problems with the Israelis," he added. The construction of Tuqu's first public building, its recently finished bright white, two-story municipal center known as the Baladyeh is a case in point. The village has an ongoing struggle with settlers and the Israeli army to keep the Baladyeh from being destroyed.

Before they forged a master plan for Tuqu', the only document the town's young managers found to start the process of determining what new projects were needed and specifically where to put them, was a recent aerial photo of the region. Such photos had been used at Oslo II to delineate the now notorious West Bank and Gaza zones A, B and C. (In Zone A were most of the major Palestinian cities under Palestinian administrative and security control; zone B was the newly created smaller Palestinian municipalities comprised of towns or villages to be administered by Palestinians but with security still under Israeli army control; zone C was the vast Israeli military security areas – more than half of the West Bank – where 99 percent of the Israeli settlements are located and whose open spaces can be closed to Palestinians at any time.)

It turns out that those photos were taken by a firm hired by Israel to make topographical pictures of the occupied territories for the Oslo II negotiations. Then the limits of the municipalities defined by Israeli negotiators were drawn meticulously and precisely on the photos by the firm's employees in thick white ink at the direction of the Israeli team and with no input from Palestinians. Summing up the arbitrary experience, the mayor said, "At Oslo the Israelis had all the advantages. They provided the data. The Palestinian negotiating team did not have detailed information, just those photomaps already marked up, which had been passed along to them from the Israeli survey department. The Palestinians at the conference could see they were being pushed, but their protests did them no good."

Ever since – all over the West Bank and Gaza – the losses because of those Israeli-imposed boundaries have been a burden. And Tuqu' is no exception. Thus when Mayor Mufarreh and his colleagues got their hands on the photomap of their area they were dismayed to discover how craftily that thick white line, which defined what was to be the municipality's Oslo-imposed perimeter, had been drawn around their village. The line had the irregular shape of an amoeba and the logic behind the perimeter's irregular path was quintessentially Israeli. The boundary line the Israeli mapmakers zealously drew around the village on the aerial photo connected all the local Palestinian homes, circa 1997, furthest from the center of the village. Everything inside that irregular, amoeba-shaped perimeter was to be zone B. Everything outside it was to be zone C, thus putting in jeopardy and subject to confiscation at any time all of the Palestinian village's agricultural land lying just outside the constricting boundary.

The inevitable effects of such gerrymandering have been to limit the area that Tuqu' needs to accommodate its increasing population (so much for a viable master plan based on the logic of expanding demographics). Also by separating the village from its surrounding agricultural lands, the Israelis have finessed the issue of ownership, making it easier to expropriate those lands.

Settlers living nearby have engaged in perpetual harassment of Tuqu's farmers as they try to work their zone C fields and orchards. Sometimes the settlers are merely threatening and intimidating, but other times they are violent. More often than not, Israeli soldiers assigned to maintain law and order look the other way while the settlers make their menacing or confiscatory moves. Sometimes the soldiers engage in their own harassing tactics.

"Settlers are willing to shoot us and get in the way of a normal life and so is the army," the mayor said. To explain, he described how Tuqu' was actually given special designation at Oslo, zone B+, "because we were big enough for a police station of our own. But we cannot control the settlers and we cannot control the army, so our police station has been closed for a long time."

Since the founding of the municipality, settlers with the acquiescence of the army have been steadily and relentlessly moving in on Tuqu', confiscating Palestinian land in the gerrymandered zone C, one field, one orchard, one olive grove at a time. In some areas along the municipal perimeter, the settlers have been frequently engaged in trying to cross the line and blatantly grab off chunks of village land and other kinds of property clearly inside zone B.

"One night settlers stole several sheep out of the village and the army did nothing to help us," said the mayor. Then both the settlers and the army came down like wolves on the village lot where the Baladyeh was proudly being built by Tuqu's residents. Recalling the community's effort and its continuing struggle to hang on to what it achieved, the mayor reminisced, "We needed a Baladyeh, but a contractor told us it would cost $300,000 to build. That was too much for us."

"So then the villagers decided, after conferring with the appropriate Palestinian Authority ministry and donors, to do as much of the work as they could by themselves without a contractor," said my friend Hisham Ali, who had brought me to Tuqu' to see the progress this once-inert village had been trying to make. I was told how the council was able to obtain $90,000 in grants from outside sources and how the village's 8,000 residents donated personal labor, materials and equipment, plus money from their own meager pockets in order to come up "with $70,000 in cash and in-kind services," said the mayor. "In the end a $300,000 building cost $160,000. Also, when we started to build it," he continued, "we made sure it was in the B zone, because according to the map, it would be sitting right on the line."

Nevertheless, as construction was nearing completion, the Israeli army ordered, "Tear it down!"

"They told us," said the mayor, "that if it's on the line, it is zone C, not zone B. Then they told us, "Since the Baladyeh is sitting on the line, it is your responsibility to remove it."

"So, the mayor went to some human rights lawyers, who went to court several times," my friend George Rishmawi added. "They helped the municipality delay the order for two or three years."

"But, even before the army interfered with us," said the mayor, "settlers started coming to the land near to where we were going to put up the Baladyeh and tried to take it from us. They told us it is famous for their religion. They said it is where the prophet Amos is buried, so they want to come to pray there." This seemed ironic since Amos, of course, was the prophet who warned the ancient Hebrews that God knew of, did not like and was being pushed to the limits of omniscient endurance by their transgressions, their sins and their tendency to push aside the needy at the gates.

"I spoke to some people and there was an investigation," the mayor continued. "I asked them, 'Where does it say in the Oslo agreement that Tuqu' is important to the religion of Israel?' They know there is nothing in the agreement about that. Then other Israelis ordered there was nothing to the claim. So the settlers stopped coming back to the land near where the Baladyeh is, at least for the time being. But since that land and the Baladyeh are at the main entrance to Tuqu', we think what the settlers really want is to control that opening," the mayor concluded.

He added that since early in 2001 the Israeli army has controlled all 21 of the village's entrances and exits. Each is blocked by high dirt barriers erected to stop automobile traffic. "It used to take me ten minutes to drive the 15 kilometers on the main roads to Bethlehem, but we do not have permission to drive on them anymore. I have to change cars three times and walk about 400 meters to get past the dirt barriers the Israeli army has built to block our side roads. Now it takes me maybe 45 minutes to an hour to get there."

The latest threat to the Baladyeh has again come from the army which insists the village never had permission to build there and never would have gotten an okay because it is in zone C. As is well known, the Israeli army is a law unto itself in the occupied territories so, despite the help from those human rights lawyers, the army can ignore—in the name of security—any orders from other Israeli officials or institutions.

"For 'security reasons' a demolition order can come at any time," said Hisham. "After that—the Baladyeh will be gone!"

"And," the mayor added, "the soldiers have warned us, 'if the army has to remove it, because you do not, you will have to pay the cost of the army taking it down.'"

"Nevertheless, despite these kinds of setbacks, which Palestinians know they can always expect from Israel, you can see that the people of Tuqu' have done much: road improvements, new schools built on land donated by local families, pipelines laid and more," George said. "It just shows what Palestinians can do when they have just a little control of their lives."

"Especially when there is motivation and persistence," Hisham interjected.

"And despite the odds," George agreed.

Then to make sure I understood exactly what he meant by "odds," George added, "spell 'odds' this way: o-c-c-u-p-a-t-i-o-n."

28

While You Were Gone
Episode 2

Hebron, West Bank, Palestine, December 19, 2003

I've written before that when we leave Palestine and Israel and head for home to renew our visas, we always hope things won't get worse here while we're gone, even knowing sadly they probably will. Unfortunately our premonitions are always correct. Since returning to the not-so-Holy Land this time, we have seen that the spirit of destruction, debilitation and depression here continues. Even in the remotest corners of the West Bank and Gaza cities, towns, villages and countryside, the dreary and gloomy monotony of Palestinian life is the norm despite the paradoxical fact of constant occupation-imposed changes that auger not relief but rather ominous, continual pain and sorrow.

Hebron's old al-Shallalah Street is one example. On one side runs the oldest of its inner-city Israeli settlements, Beit Hadassah, and on the other a long row of first-floor Palestinian shops with Palestinian apartments above them. When the Israeli army extended its control over H2 by appropriating a piece of H1, al-Shallalah Street was more adversely affected than some others swallowed up in the same unilateral redrawing of the West Bank map. Because it was no longer in the more vigorous H1 commercial and residential area, al-Shallalah Street's business and personal life made a catastrophic nosedive. Not only did the tiny neighborhood have to endure the constant curfews that were the terrible lot of Palestinians living in H2, but also it was ruled off-limits to anyone except those who actually lived there.

To recap, H1 is the area of Hebron with some 105,000 Palestinians living in it which was granted by the post-Oslo Wye River Accords to the Palestinian National Authority but then was reoccupied by Israel in the summer of 2002. At the Wye River negotiations, Israelis insisted that an area of Hebron called H2 be assigned to Israel because it is home to a unique enclave of four small ultra-orthodox, ultranationalist Jewish settlements. In H2 approximately 450 militant residents, backed by some 2,000 Israeli soldiers at any one time (over against H2's 45,000 Palestinians who have no one to protect them) have over the years been stunningly successful at stifling and closing down most Palestinian business inside the Old City as well as creating such discouraging conditions that more than half the Palestinian population has fled.

Actually, life stopped being sweet in al-Shallalah Street long before it was unilaterally made part of H2 last year. The bad days began and became a way of life when Beit Hadassah was established more than two decades ago. Militant settler residents, often joined by belligerent ultranationalists not necessarily from West Bank settlements, rampaged virtually unhindered in and above the narrow street and harassed shopkeepers and residents. They damaged or destroyed merchandise or, from Beit Hadassah windows above the street, pelted passersby with refuse, garbage, slop and also more dangerous objects like rocks, tiles and cement blocks while Israeli police, border police or soldiers stood by to ensure that no settlers were harmed in return. The Israeli army's subsequent worse-than-the-disease antidote to the violence was—in the wake of such attacks—to order the shops closed, imposing a curfew in the street to "protect" the Palestinians.

Finally came the de facto annexation into H2 that actually made the street into a blockade even to its residents who were grudgingly allowed to leave and return, especially when there was curfew. Then suddenly late last month the blockade was lifted. Palestinians were once more allowed to come and go and conduct business as they pleased. Almost immediately, although street rampages have been successfully prevented by the various Israeli security forces in Hebron, the dangerous bombardments from Beit Hadassah windows above the street began again.

Occupation authorities have, however, quickly moved to thwart the danger, not by arresting settler provocateurs but by installing a transparent metallic mesh net along the entire length of al-Shallalah Street between the first- and second-floor level to keep the angry missiles dropped from above from reaching the streets. Walking beneath it the other day, I could see among the trapped debris above me a two-foot long slab of cement. The street is never going to be what it once was—an exuberant, boisterous neighborhood of thriving shops and homes. Since our return to Hebron on December 15, I have checked on this forlorn street almost daily but have yet to see one open shop or a single Palestinian resident either coming or going.

So much for the city. Out in the country east of Hebron, along with other CPTers and internationals, I was led recently to a towering mound of rock and stone "fill" that is growing ominously higher and higher just outside the northern edge of the West Bank's oldest Israeli settlement, Kiryat Arba. Purposefully being dumped onto adjacent Palestinian farmland in a shallow valley called Wadi al-Ghroos, it is a looming presence marking the latest incremental phase in the settlement's ongoing landgrab at the expense of its Palestinian neighbors. The "fill" is being used to surface 35-foot-wide dirt swaths being bulldozed farther and farther down into and over the valley's fields, orchards and vineyards. Once surfacing has been completed, high-wire fences equipped with electronic sensors will be installed for—according to the settlers—"security reasons." According to Palestinians, whose livelihood-supporting property is being wrested from them, the roads and fences are being built, like those in the past, so the settlers can "steal our land."

There is, of course, a factual element to both views. Security for the settlers is an issue because the former protective buffer "security" strip of land previously confiscated from Wadi al-Ghroos Palestinians situated just outside the settlement's former outer ring of housing has disappeared beneath a long row of recently built settler homes. So a replacement buffer security zone for this new outer ring is now in the process of being created. A historic sameness to this process of change exists, just as it does in the strangling of the Hebron neighborhood described above.

Each time a new expansion takes place, Wadi al-Ghroos farmers are promised that once work is completed they will have access to their former plots, but in practice this never has proved to be the case. In fact, once the work begins, armed settlers prevent them from being on their property, so during the past year some 50 *dunams* of land at the northwest corner of Kiryat Arba was lost to the farmers. Recently bulldozers began leveling paths for even newer graveled roads along which more of those fences with their electronic sensors will be built, paving the way for the isolation of another 50 *dunams* along the settlements' northern edge.

As settlement boundaries are pushed out from Kiryat Arba into Wadi al-Ghroos, the affected families have lodged official complaints, through lawyers, with the local office of the civil administration. But those civilian functionaries actually work for Israel's Ministry of Defense – the sole and inevitably arbitrary ruler of the occupied territories. These employees are only superficially civil. Like death and taxes and despite lower court victories in connection with these kinds of land seizures, at the end of the day the Palestinians, more often than not, lose.

So in the current dispute, even though the Israeli army has temporarily halted bulldozing, it is not restraining the continued buildup of that growing mound of rock and stone "fill." As dump trucks continue unhindered to add to the pile, expectations are, as in the past, that more Wadi al-Ghroos' farmland, which has been lovingly and thankfully worked for generations by its Palestinian residents, is destined to end up beyond their reach and benefit— behind brand-new, unilaterally assigned borders and boundaries that mark off an ever-shrinking map of Palestine.

29

"Mirror, Mirror on the Wall"

Hebron, West Bank, Palestine, January 6, 2004

While wading through responses to one of my latest reports, I came across the following refutation. "Part of the problem that nobody talks about is the Palestinian educational system that instills hostility and hatred from early grade school on, [and] doctrines that lead to suicide homicides."

My answer to that familiar refrain is: even though this reputed cornerstone of Palestinian teaching is certainly talked about repeatedly in some quarters such as AIPAC or the *Jerusalem Post*, I want to know: What's really to talk about?

What does need to be talked about is that Palestinian youngsters don't need their schools to "instill hostility and hatred" of Israel (or a series of U.S.-complicit administrations for that matter) because if they really needed such education, it would mean they had been sleeping through the daily experiences of the debilitating and demeaning Occupation. No Palestinian can escape that, awake or asleep.

Specifically what they can't escape is the kind of Israeli hostility and hatred (of which ironically only the Palestinians are being accused) in the form of soldiers and settlers in their midst, whose continued presence provides irrefutable assurance that escalating

annexation of their land will continue; that a variety of non-judi-
cial collective punishments for daring to oppose the occupation
will continue – like imprisonment without charges in the form of
curfews, detentions or jailings of thousands of boys, men, girls and
women, as well as President Arafat; that home demolitions and the
withholding, theft and thwarting of such services and essentials as
water, electricity, medicine, clinics and hospitals will continue; that
the severest restrictions of movement of goods and people from
village to village and town to town anywhere in the world will
continue; and that in the Old City of Hebron, CPT will need to
continue – apparently indefinitely – to conduct its daily school patrols in order to be on the spot when settlers and soldiers try to
stop youngsters from trying to get an education.

Furthermore, having experienced the U.S. educational system
firsthand, I find that instilling chauvinistic antagonisms, national
and racial condescensions, jingoistic and tainted concepts of history, fomenting violence and rationalizing politically correct patriotism is not much different than what is being taught elsewhere in
the world, including the Middle East and especially Israel, which
as we know, outside of the U.S., is the most extensively militarized
nation in the world – an authentic Goliath pitted against a Palestinian David.

As for "doctrines that lead to suicide homicides," if the writer
meant a so-called technique of incitement that reportedly promises
recruits the prospect of sleeping with a bevy of beautiful virgins
in Paradise, such assurances are simply the Middle Eastern version
of recruiting incentives applied everywhere. For instance, in the
U.S. where sleeping around this side of paradise is an easier propo-
sition for libidinous young American males than for their Middle
Eastern counterparts, the remarkably similar recruitment assurance
to American prospects is still that they, too, can be all that they
want to be.

However, given the circumstances of every young Palestinian's
dreary existence, when it comes to sleeping in paradise, the other
day my wife Sis wondered: If the promise of multiple sex with

multiple virgins in Paradise is really what is convincing young Palestinians to become suicide bombers and not the desperate existence they are still being obliged to endure, then how come young Palestinian women have been willing to die that way, too?

Of course, in writing this, I am creating the possibility of being misunderstood with respect to the purported efficacy of violence – a grave notion which runs counter to my belief. So, I add the following disclaimer to the preceding arguments: I am neither excusing nor rationalizing the terrible effects of "suicide homicides." What I have said must not be taken as an apologetic for today's violent Palestinian terrorists, but, of course, the same condemnation applies to their terrorizing Israeli army counterparts.

Moreover, those critical of Palestinian violence, especially suicidal violence, in order to discredit Palestinian aspirations for genuine independence, cannot have it both ways. Let's remember that acts of desperation-driven suicidal violence are an honored component of Israeli lore too. Remember Samson? And then several hundred years later there was the mass murder of the cornered women and children by their Zealot husbands and fathers atop the Masada mountaintop in the Judean wilderness. This hallowed event – taught as the epitome of honorable patriotism – took place during the final desperate days of a Jewish revolt against Rome. Then, in an act of terminal defiance, the male remnant committed suicide rather than be taken prisoner. One wonders what those ancient heroes promised their loved ones with respect to a paradise to come as they slit the throats of their wives and children.

Some will complain that I have my nerve – to perceive a symmetry that really doesn't exist between those long-ago events and what today's purportedly lust-driven Palestinian youngsters have been perpetrating on Israeli innocents during the current uprising. Perhaps there isn't. But I do perceive an undeniable asymmetry. So let's leave it at that.

30

We Get Letters

Hebron, West Bank, Palestine, January 9, 2004

My last missive reacting to a writer's accusation about the Palestinian educational system drew an unusually extensive range of thoughtful responses. It seemed appropriate to incorporate some of those thoughts here. Since the writers have not been asked for permission to make their reactions public, I won't include names. Plus a tiny bit of editing has been done for compression and clarity.

Working backward through my piece, here are three comments concerning my critique of the "asymmetrical" connection between Masada and current suicide attacks.

1) "Among many other things I love in [your] report is that it is the only place I have ever seen in print that Masada was not a 'mass suicide' but a brutal murder of women, children and other men by a group of men selected for this purpose. Finally someone is saying it aloud."

2) "I was especially struck by the mention of Masada because it reminded me of the horror I felt in learning of how Jewish parents killed their own children and then themselves in the European ghettos rather than convert. I remember thinking that surely there could have been a better way."

3) "I don't think it's useful to cite ancient Jewish history as somehow relevant to this conflict. This plays into the notion that there is a sort of ancient conflict that's been going on since 'time immemorial' – as well as an echoing of Zionist ideology which incorporates such religious stories to reinforce Jewish claims to the land. I think it's important to note that this is not a religious conflict. Religion is exploited – by all sides – for political ends, but it is fundamentally a political conflict."

As to what motivates suicide attacks today, here are three opinions:

1) "What's hardest to stomach is the contrast between suicide bombers and our Apache pilots who wash away other people's blood with a shower and a beer."

2) "As your analysis demonstrates, sex with virgins is not the main reason Palestinians commit suicide operations, but your reference itself is a bit of a stereotype. Many of the suicide bombers aren't even religious (and neither are some groups – like the PFLP (Progressive Party for the Liberation of Palestine). Many became 'religious' just before carrying out their mission. Several of them, as you noted, are also women. I think it's important to debunk the stereotype of the sexually repressed Muslim fanatical male looking to quench his sexual appetite. Obsessive Western references to the houris only play up this stereotype while reflecting Orientalist-Western misnomers about Islam.

"I thought the parallels you drew between recruitment methods there and elsewhere in the world were much more useful – and very apt. In fact sex is a more powerful recruitment method for American servicemen than Palestinians, as our military bases abroad often fund entire sex industries to 'service' our soldiers (e.g. Korea, the Philippines, etc.) – to say nothing of the rampant sexual abuse and rape that goes unabated within the U.S. military itself."

3) "I agree with 95% of what you say. However, if I dare say, to me you still sound like an apologist... Remember that the men who flew the planes into the Twin Towers, the Pentagon and into the ground were from good backgrounds, had good educations,

were not poor and were not Palestinian.... It's Islam turned into a death cult that led these suicide killer-hijackers and pilots to do what they did and so it is with many Palestinian bombers – note that at least one suicide bomber that struck Israel was an Egyptian.... The promise of 72 virgins must, to some extent, be a driving force behind what they do.... As for the women who carry out these attacks, they still believe that in some way they will get their reward in paradise though it is not clearly said in the Koran.... You can't negotiate with people like this."

Finally, with respect to the claim that Palestinian schools teach hostility and hatred:

1) "[About] your point that one doesn't need books or classes.... The 24-hour assault on every normal activity in Palestine is living testimony to the violence of the occupation."

2) "The [Palestinian] curriculum is set and approved by the Israeli authorities. These schools can only teach what the Israeli government tells them to teach. So, it is a little rich to hear the accusation that schools are teaching Palestinian children to become suicide bombers, especially when such false accusations are positively encouraged by the Israeli authorities. In the Lutheran hostel in Jaffa I met [someone who] was spouting this nonsense. I told her not to be such a fool as to swallow the Israeli propaganda so easily. I think I upset her."

3) [The writer was] totally misinformed. I am working here with the very Palestinian school system which he erroneously describes. I have just left a major international conference of academics in Jerusalem who were discussing (among other things) just such malicious (however misguided) manipulation of the public...- especially in the U.S....with the obvious aim of justifying and building continued support [for] the state of Israel as it continues illegal, violent oppression of the Palestinian people living under its cruel occupation. The sad fact to me was observing all of the distinguished Jewish academics participating (both Israelis and internationals) who were deeply distressed, even horrified, at this type of intellectual, not to mention moral blasphemy."

4) "When one lives within the brutal constraints that are being applied to 'everyday' Palestinians, life in the raw is the key 'educational system' for whatever may be instilled regarding 'hostility.' ... My impression is that radical elements connected to certain mosques would be the more likely venues for any 'instilling' or even the subtle recruiting that goes on in Palestine."

5) "We went to a Methodist church to hear Alex Awad speak. After his presentation...one man asked 'If Palestinians want peace so badly, why do Palestinian textbooks still teach children to hate Israelis?' [This was after having been given] the facts regarding the dates that ALL such teachings were removed from the textbooks. Alex said, 'Palestinian children need no textbooks to teach hate; they only have to look out their window each morning when they get up and see the tanks and military presence everywhere. Most children have witnessed housing demolitions, farmland and ancient olive trees bulldozed, as well as a family member or friend shot by a sniper. Who needs a textbook?' The man had no more questions."

6) "You provided a much-needed correction to the common, ridiculous notion that Palestinians somehow have to be taught to hate the people who are brutally oppressing them. I might add, though – as you yourself will surely attest – that I was and continue to be floored by how many Palestinians do not hate the people who are oppressing them – who simply want them to leave their land finally so they can found their state and live 'like siblings' side by side."

31

Bad Fences Don't Make Good Neighbors

Hebron, West Bank, Palestine, January 28, 2004

As W.C. Fields once said, "It's time to take the bull by the tail and face the situation." If the so-called "separation" or "security" fence that the Likud government is building – not just around but well *into* the West Bank – was only being constructed for mutually benign purposes leading to the resolution of territorial issues and achieving a kind of security for both Israelis and Palestinians, then best wishes to its builders. But that never was, has not been and is not the case today. With respect to the issue of security, the intent is one-sided, to say the least. With respect to the issue of territorial integrity, again the intent is, to say the very least, defiant.

To begin with: the fence is not a fence as in "a rose is a rose is a rose." In many places along its astonishing route it is an approximately 25-foot-high concrete barrier/wall.

However, beware!

If one gets swept into debating the issue of whether this is a fence or a wall, it diverts international attention from the serious, sinister and clearly malign political context of the "wall." I first began reporting on the effect of this barrier last year. In the interim, sad to say, more now than ever we need to shout from the housetops – Demosthenes-like – "Beware of Sharon of Israel!" Notwithstanding President Bush's near-toothless critical description last summer of Israel's unilateral land expropriation process being pushed deeper and deeper into the heart of the West Bank ("snaking" President Bush called it), the annexation process has proceeded at such a voracious pace that original estimates of the hugeness of the land-grab have been wildly exceeded. Israel's latest official map (www.securityfence.mod.gov.il/Pages/ENG/route.htm) with the route clearly delineated reveals that almost 15 percent (about 210,000 acres) of Palestinian land lying east of the Green Line has been swallowed up without benefit of negotiation. Last year at this time the estimate was ten percent.

Clearly after the Israeli snake of land-confiscation shed its post-Camp David II skin, it emerged bigger, more venomous and with more powerful jaws than ever before. In some places the eastward penetration is 22 kilometers. According to a UN report issued in December (*United Nations Office for the Coördination of Humanitarian Affairs: Occupied Palestinian Territory 15 December 2003*), 400,000 Palestinians living on the West Bank side of the wall will need to cross through a limited number of checkpoints and gates to get to their farms, jobs and services. Those who have stood in line with Palestinians trying to move from even Bethlehem to Jerusalem or into and out of Nablus these days through similar Israeli checkpoints – often in the rain – know what an often-futile, terribly slow and utterly humiliating time-consuming ordeal that can be.

True to form and past practice, getting through the "annexation" wall delineating these newly expropriated regions will be the result of unpredictable official whim which, more than any other characteristic, seems to govern the Israeli's army control and operation of the openings in the wall. Each day 30 percent of the total West Bank Palestinian population is being adversely affected because of this regular uncertainty.

Conversely, 113,000 Palestinians who previously lived in Palestine now find themselves residing on Palestinian land newly annexed by the wall into Israel proper and saddled with restrictions affecting travel, economic and physical survival – which are more onerous than before. Entire Palestinian villages lying inside the newly annexed Israeli territory are being encircled by second walls with limited access – much like those around gated communities in a number of Western nations. The significant difference, however, is that in the free West, unlike unfree Palestine, gated communities are designed by their well-off residents to keep rascals and riffraff out, whereas here it appears the gated communities are built by rascals and riffraff to lock the not-so-well-off Palestinians in. Explain to me the difference between these and the ghettos in Warsaw.

So what we have here is not a mutually acceptable wall built to ensure security for two separate and equally viable states – Israeli and Palestinian – whose limits were delineated by the internationally sanctioned and multilaterally agreed-upon 1949 border known as the Green Line. Rather it is a disingenuous Israeli-road-map-be-scorned, Taba-Talks-be-scorned, Camp-David-II-be-scorned, Oslo-be-scorned, UN-Security-Council-Resolution-242-(among others)-be-scorned "annexation" fence/wall-building process – audaciously and unilaterally laid out to enhance what was once described by *New York Times* columnist Thomas Friedman as Israel's "insane landgrab."

The effect of this nightmarish end-run around diplomatic conflict resolution with respect to political finality is likely to be the same as the result of Israel's unilateral annexation just after the 1967 war when it took many square miles of Palestinian land bordering Jerusalem on the north, east and south. This enlarged Jerusalem became the nucleus of the several-mile-wide, Israeli-only corridor that quite effectively cut the West Bank in two and became the genesis of the issue of non-contiguity, newly inflamed these days by the wall – a significant issue which has been clouding the viability of Palestinian statehood ever since.

Since the wall began moving eastward into Palestine rather than south along the Green Line two summers ago – uprooting Palestinian olive trees and groves in its path, as well as confiscating Palestinian farmland, cutting off Palestinian villages and towns from their water supply and surrounding fields – the pace of the non-contiguous "snaking" has increased. By now Palestine is divided de facto into several unconnected sections instead of the original two. This non-contiguity was one of the fundamental building blocks of former Israeli Prime Minister Barak's famous (notorious?) "generous offer" at Camp David II in the summer of 2000 – the Barak so-called 98 percent of the West Bank generous-offer-that-never-was.

Despite the craftiness of that aspect of the Labor Party leader's "generosity," an overlooked element of the Barak proposals dealt with zone C where over half of the Palestinian area in the West Bank, according to the Oslo agreements, has remained under indefinite Israeli military control and rule. On paper this major portion of zone C that was granted to the Palestinians was supposedly to be the subject of future post-Camp-David negotiations, but the talks have never taken place. So the Israeli military continues its absolute despotic rule characterized by continued confiscation of ominously larger tracts of prime farmland and wells in the areas surrounding most settlements. Home demolitions and "preventative" harassment continues as Palestinian farmers try vainly to work their shrinking acreage.

No wonder Arafat (his well-publicized faults in much of the Israel-mostly-right-and-hardly-wrong indulgent international press notwithstanding) walked away from Camp David. Just stop for a moment and imagine what would have happened if George Washington, after the battle of Yorktown, had accepted from King George the same kind of "generous" offer that Barak – seconded by President Clinton – is endlessly reported to have pushed at Arafat. Do you suppose that a royal proposal depicted on an 18th century royal map which, while supposedly embracing the notion of peaceful "separation" from Britain and viable statehood for the colonies, actually divided them into three non-contiguous zones for – according to the king – "security" reasons. His map could have shown the New England states "separated" from the Middle Atlantic States by a few-miles-wide "security" corridor to be controlled indefinitely by the Red Coats and the Mid-Atlantic states "separated" from the Southern states by a similar English-controlled corridor. What do you suppose would have happened to Washington if he had taken such an offer to the Continental Congress for ratification?

Probably the same thing that would have happened to Arafat if he had taken Barak's so-called generous offer, the Camp David II map, to the Palestinian National Authority.

32

Seeing the Forest as Well as the Trees

Hebron, West Bank, Palestine, February 4, 2004

I received a critical reaction to my last commentary. I share it as an example of how one can carelessly miss the forest because of the trees and thus convey an unintended insensitivity.

Now, I don't mean my critic missed the forest. I missed it!

First of all, in truncated form, what motivated his reaction was an analogy I used to illustrate my argument that Arafat had no choice but to walk away from Camp David II: "Imagine what would have happened to George Washington, if after the battle of Yorktown, he had accepted from King George the kind of "generous" offer [Israeli Prime Minister] Barak pushed at Arafat. Imagine a royal proposal showing 1) the New England states "separated" from the Middle Atlantic States by a "security" corridor to be controlled indefinitely by the Red Coats, and 2) the Middle Atlantic States "separated" from the Southern States by a similar England-controlled corridor. Can you imagine what would have happened to Washington, if he had taken such an offer to the Continental Congress? Probably the same thing that would have happened to Arafat if he had taken the so-called generous offer Barak made to the Palestinian National Authority."

Now here's what my perceptive critic, who lives in Tennessee, had to say. "I would suggest that your analogies need to be reëxamined. To compare the Palestinians to the American colonialists is nonsymmetry.... The American colonialists, just like the Zionist movement, came to a land of native population. The Palestinians, therefore, are not analogous to the colonists, but rather to the Native American population that continues to be subjugated and oppressed in their own homeland."

My first reaction (not conveyed to the writer, I'm relieved to report) was, sad to say, knee-jerk defensive. With respect to his barb concerning "nonsymmetry," my initial thought was to plead asymmetry (as I have done on other occasions). But then I decided that even if his assault on my analogy had spilled considerable wind from its sails, to debate his point on those grounds would have been an unproductive hairsplitting exercise in pedantry. It also might have initiated an even more serious diversion from the intentional consideration of a consequential variety of truths that are stranger than facts.

After all, he was making a compelling point, one I often have echoed when speaking to audiences back home in the States. It goes something like this:

"More than one Palestinian and Israeli human-rights activist has asked Sis and me plaintively, 'Why does America treat Palestinians like its Native Americans?' Of course, that treatment does not compute for us either, although as Americans, Sis and I do think we comprehend the malign motivations, which are ascendant here at home, in a way that some Palestinians and their Israeli supporters find it hard to grasp. And the answer is mind-boggling.

"Why does America treat Palestinians like its Native Americans? Our answer, sadly, is always this: 'Because that's what America does! Get it? That's what America does.'"

In light of that conclusion, my critic's point is vital. The Revolutionary War, important as it was for the colonists, was a shot across British bows that was more analogous (and a prediction of things to come) to the Boer War than it was to Palestine's struggle with Zionism or the Ghandhian struggle against British colonialism.

Despite my "that's what America does," truth, what continues to amaze me is how incredibly indulgent non-Americans are to us, even when fully aware of the agonizing historic and contemporary contradiction in the American character. Our overseas friends, continuing to make a distinction between our government and the rest of us, more often than not will say to us, "We don't hate Americans, we love America. We just don't like what your government is doing."

Which is far more credit than many Americans will give to non-Americans. Thus the attractiveness amongst too many Americans of the pernicious notion that all Arabs are terrorists.

Pondering the awfulness of that truth suddenly reminded me of the following anecdote from our travels about the States which I should have remembered when I was comparing a fanciful Yorktown aftermath to Camp David II.

Sis and I left our hometown, Birmingham, Alabama, and headed east on a speaking tour the day after the September 11, 2001 attack that destroyed the World Trade Center. At the end of that week we were in New York where we shared our experiences with an intercultural group, the Westchester County Peace Action Committee, a venerable organization dedicated to nonviolence with a membership consisting of Jews, Christians, Muslims, Hindus, Buddhists, Native Americans and others. The main topic of worried discussion that night was the post-destruction backlash already afflicting Muslims and Christian Arabs across the country, and what to do about it.

There came an existential moment, when a tall, powerful man with long jet-black hair, unmistakably a Native American, shared his ironically cogent thoughts. To begin with, he told us he is a direct descendant of a Lakota Sioux leader at the battle of Little Big Horn, also known as the site of *Custer's Last Stand*. "After that," he said, "my family renounced violence."

These days, he told us, he is a repairman for a big East Coast utility. The morning after the attack, he was sent to an upscale home to make repairs. "When the owner took a look at me, he insisted on examining my tool box. 'Never can be too careful, these days,'" our new friend said the owner told him "nervously" – not apologetically.

Later another homeowner – again unapologetically – insisted on scrutinizing, through a locked screen door, the picture on our new friend's company ID.

After that he took a coffee break at a local truck stop popular with other "hard hats," where he hoped to recover from those unsettling encounters.

"But it was just my luck to sit near two men who were talking very loudly and angrily. They were doing it in a way that indicated clearly they wanted their thoughts about what ought to be done about the attack to be heard by everyone in the restaurant. One said pointedly and very harshly – '*We* ought to extradite all of *them*!!!' (Even though it was clear he didn't know what extradite meant, there was no doubt in my mind about who *we* and *them* were.)"

Our repairman friend went on to say, "The other hard hat in an equally loud voice agreed saying, 'Yeah, *we* ought to send them all back to where *they* came from.'"

"After that, I knew I had to do something. But I also knew it had to be in keeping with my nonviolent convictions. Now, I could see that I was much bigger than they were, so – to try to get their attention – I slowly stood up and kind of sauntered over to where they were sitting. I got it. They stopped talking and kind of waited to see what was going to happen next. I stepped up real close so that they could not mistake who and what I was.

"Then looming over them – not quite in their faces – I said very quietly but quite emphatically, 'You know, that's a damn good idea.'"

33

The Sad Sounds of Silence

Hebron, West Bank, Palestine, February 25, 2004

A fundamental CPT undertaking in Hebron is to give the never-ending stream of fact-seeking visitors from around the world exploratory tours of its dying Old City. We do this to help them comprehend the extent of the harm and continual peril to Palestinian lives and livelihood that goes on in the heart of Hebron's once-thriving commercial and residential area.

The flourishing campaign of debilitation and dispossession going on here is a microcosmic reflection of the incredible energy and dynamism of the crusade of dispossession and destruction waged by Israel throughout the West Bank, especially in areas around Jerusalem and Bethlehem. There, less than two years ago, a stupendous rush of construction produced the "annexation" wall/ fence. Unilaterally, Zionists began what may be their final land-greedy push to absorb "occupied territories" into Israel. "Annexation" walls like those in the northern and central areas of the West Bank have not yet begun to go up in the south, but the effects of the relentless house-by-house, shop-by-shop expansion of the perimeter around the tiny Israeli settlements congregated in the heart of Hebron's Old City have been essentially the same.

In reality what has happened here in Hebron (and elsewhere in the West Bank) has not been a "peace process," but a "piece process." A Palestinian friend of CPT's got it right when she talked about the practice of de facto annexation masquerading as separation as "Israel taking a piece of Palestine here, a piece of Palestine there and another piece of Palestine here again...."

Hebron's tiny Israeli settlements are located in Israeli-army-ruled H2, but the process of gradual and continual confiscation of Palestinian Old City homes and shop space adjacent to the settlements began long before the Oslo Accords and has been, to say the least, provocative. Spates of settler rampages through adjoining Palestinian neighborhoods triggered violent protests inevitably and retaliation, followed by Israeli military counteraction which would put all Palestinians of H2 under long curfews in order to "protect the Arabs from the settlers." No such would-be pacifying measure was ever imposed on Israeli settlers.

The pace of confiscation by Israelis actually quickened and has become steadily more debilitating since the second uprising began. At any one time there are over 2,000 Israeli soldiers, border and local police separating the 450 Israeli settlers from their approximately 45,000 Palestinians neighbors in H2 who are still trying to hang on. Meanwhile the settlers protected by the Israeli military and police are constantly finding new ways to expand their domain by pushing out Palestinians. So to help visitors visualize the catastrophic effects of "piece processing" in Hebron, CPT's tours often begin in the city's Manara section, about a mile north of the settlements in order for the fact-finders to contrast what they see and hear there with what they will later encounter around the Israeli settlements in the Old City.

Manara is in H1 – the part of the city with 105,000 Palestinians living there that was granted by the Wye River Accords in 1997 to the Palestinian National Authority. But two summers ago, Israel reoccupied Manara. Making our way through the noisy outdoor market clogging Manara's network of H1 feeder streets, we have to shout to be heard over the perpetual din of shoppers packing the sidewalks and boisterous shopkeepers yelling out their wares. There was the continual obbligato of automobile horns pounded impatiently by frustrated drivers of taxis, jitneys, buses, private automobiles and trucks – all trying to snake their way through the crowd of pedestrians vying for the same turf.

Another ten-minute walk takes us to Bab iZaweyya, another major crossroads half-way to the Old City which until late December 2002 was as hectically busy as Manara is these days. Manara and Bab iZaweyya have reversed roles, for now this junction is empty because businesses here were virtually bankrupted when the Israeli army unilaterally pushed the post-Wye River Accords border between H1 and H2 a quarter of mile into H1 territory, stopping at a line just north of Bab iZaweyya. Thus, touring visitors crossing the boundary into de facto H2, encounter an increasingly desolate and deserted commercial cityscape marked by large waist-high heavy cement cubes blocking the streets. Pedestrian traffic drops to a trickle. Vehicles, except those belonging to the Israeli military or police, are not permitted. There is no problem being heard, even if one whispers. Shopkeepers stand or sit listlessly in front of their stores waiting for business that has dwindled away.

The noise of human activity drops even further as the group moves through a major Israeli checkpoint, Beit Romano, adjacent to a several-stories-high Orthodox settler yeshiva looming over that end of the Old City. We continue our walk through a small plaza surrounded on three sides by Palestinian shops, none open, which marks the northern entrance to the Old City's once-thriving residential and market area. Two years ago this tiny piece of Palestinian real estate was full of vigorous life and most of its two dozen shops were still open for business. Now the plaza is gritty, dusty, trash-strewn and abandoned. The apartments above are just as empty as the shops and many of the other buildings the visitors pass during the rest of their quarter-mile trek through the Old City. Most have been deserted because of the settler's rampages and subsequent military indifference to the Palestinians' plight.

The roof of the Old City building where the CPT apartment is housed is a good spot from which to get a panoramic view of the intensely troubled and slowly dying area. I usually start by facing visitors north where they can look down on a small Israeli army outpost a block away, located in what was once Hebron's busy central bus station. Because of the outpost, we are forbidden to take pictures facing in that direction. To emphasize the prohibition, I point out two small Israeli military rooftop outposts across the street from us at either end of a row of abandoned apartment buildings. We know the soldiers stationed there keep an eye on what happens here because usually if someone takes a picture facing the army outpost, by the time they have walked down the steps from the apartment into the street, soldiers are waiting outside poised to confiscate their film or memory card.

No matter what direction one looks from the roof, the lifelessness of the Old City strikes you. A sense of gloom and malaise prevails, especially when compared to the energy and vitality you experience just a few blocks to the north in Manara. The faint street sounds beneath the CPT apartment are typical of all Palestinian shopping streets in the Old City. A once-busy poultry market, where cackling geese and crowing roosters were a normal part of the daily din created by chattering shoppers and shopkeepers, is deserted most of the time now.

Until early last year, Palestinians still shopped there, as did CPT. But not any more. The steel doors to the several shops with their coops for the flocks of poultry or pens for the occasional rabbit being readied for market are rarely opened. When they are, it is only so the proprietors can feed the animals and birds or bring in replacements for those removed and transported to the few shops still open for business elsewhere in the Old City or further away in H1. Last year a handful of Palestinian families still lived in apartments above the shops. Today, except for CPT, every family has fled.

Settlers-only Shuhada Street just to the west of the CPT apartment building is empty most of the time except for an occasional car, military or police vehicle, or Israeli bus ending its regular run down from Jerusalem's central bus station or about to start back. To the north a settler or two may be seen occasionally, walking along Shuhada Street on the way to or from one of the two tiny settlements located there: Beit Hadassah or Tel Rumeida.

The only Palestinians allowed to walk here are the few who have tenaciously hung on, but they must live under lonely and degrading circumstances. Their friends and family who live in H1 or elsewhere are not allowed to visit. Residents themselves must pass through an Israeli checkpoint every time they leave or return to their neighborhood; and the frightening and often injurious or destructive harassment by settlers is a constant. To the south toward Avraham Avinu, the last of the inner-city settlements, there is little activity in the street there, too. Occasionally a settler car heads toward Kiryat Arba – the big settlement perched behind Hebron's eastern ridge – perhaps to shop there or pass through on its way to Jerusalem – an easy half-hour drive away if you're an Israeli.

When I first came to Hebron about 18 years ago, its main commercial area was the Old City and many of its main markets were on Shuhada Street where all the inner-city settlements are now congregated. Back then during business hours the area was even more crowded than Manara is today because besides local shoppers there were tourists – hundreds of them – pouring into the Old City each day on foot, as well as on those big, rumbling tourist buses competing with local traffic for street space. All in all, it was an exuberantly noisy place. Today many of the vendors loudly hawking their wares – arranged on tabletops lining the streets in Manara – are merchants who once owned prosperous stores in the Old City which they could lock up at night. Now they must take everything down at the end of the day, cart it away, lock it up in some nearby storeroom and then set it all up again the next day.

Whenever I take visitors to our roof, I always ask them to "Listen – just listen to the sounds of the Old City and tell me what you hear." After 30 seconds or so of straining to hear what I'm pointing out to them, they usually give me a blank stare. So I repeat, "So, what do you hear?"

Some of the visitors look confused or unsure as how to respond until one finally will say in a hesitant, almost questioning, tone. "Nothing?"

"Exactly!" I say. "Now you know how to go home and begin to tell the story of Hebron's dying Old City..."

34

"Now the Sun Sets at 2:30"

Hebron, West Bank, Palestine, April 7, 2004

Once again, coming back to Palestine hoping that things won't be worse than when we left, but actually knowing they can be, we nevertheless are sad to find our hopes dashed. This time we left in early March on a quickie speaking tour of the UK and then returned to Bethlehem and Hebron at the end of the month. Usually our trips away are longer, but despite the short hiatus, the situation in Hebron darkened considerably during those brief three weeks.

Even before we left, the daily micro-struggles around our area which CPT took part in or witnessed had added up to minus progress toward achieving Palestinian freedom and changing the debilitating effects of the occupation. This desperate state of affairs, echoed in every corner of the shrinking Palestinian West Bank map, added up to macro-distress and pervasive chronic despair throughout the occupied territories. Several kilometers to the north of Hebron, evidence of the tightening Israeli (U.S.-enabled) noose around Palestine continued with the nonstop cancer-like absorption of West Bank farmlands and homesteads. The landgrab included property lying inside Israeli military security zone C and also the steady incorporation of Palestinian property lying clearly inside the boundaries of Palestinian cities and towns comprising zones A and B. These too had become part of the expanding Israeli land mass lying west of the ever-lengthening "annexation" wall.

The ever-changing map of this new contiguous "greater Israel" continued to be defined by each new acre of Palestinian land covered over by the wall. Conversely the barrier's unilaterally ordered (and – to a shameful degree – unilaterally U.S.-enabled) path also identified the latest non-contiguous limits of the shrinking map of a "lesser" Palestine. For every acre of Palestinian territory that ended up on the "wrong" side of the wall, the amount of Palestinian suffering increased proportionally. Thus Palestinians or internationals trying to get through a major checkpoint blocking the old Hebron Road leading into Bethlehem from the north watched helplessly during their long waits as a nearby major earth-moving project took shape. They are powerless to stop the wide path on confiscated Palestinian land where the wall is going to be built. Eventually it will separate a northern Bethlehem neighborhood from the municipality and at least double the size of the expropriated area around Rachel's tomb that Israel annexed to Jerusalem a few years ago.

Meanwhile, the 29-foot high concrete wall slicing through Abu Dis in the East Jerusalem area cuts off Al-Quds University from its students and faculty who live inside the city. Because of the well-known Palestinian desire to learn and teach, this obscene barrier has created an always-inconvenient, sometimes-perilous route for those compelled to find ways to sneak from one side of the wall to the other to pursue their education or academic livelihood. The wall snakes south past the university up to the top of a nearby hill where it separates homes on the eastern Palestinian side from unbuilt-up Palestinian areas to the west.

Besides limiting growth, this high wall creates another, piteously unique problem for villagers living in its shadow. "Now," one depressed villager told me, "the sun sets at 2:30." Another villager, overhearing his neighbor's sad commentary, added, "Now the Israelis have put a curfew on the sun."

With respect to curfews and given my view that every day in almost every way the quality of Palestinian life under the occupation is worsening, it may seem contradictory to report that since late fall the imposition of curfews has almost stopped; but that is not a contradiction.

There, is, I believe, a not-very-acceptable reason for this seeming inconsistency. The Sharon-led government is winning its ideological and political struggle to defeat the notion of – as well as the actuality of – any kind of logistically feasible and viable Palestinian state. Both Sharon and his defense minister Mofaz know it because – except for suicide bombings and occasional guerilla attacks which are not succeeding in loosening the tightening Israeli grip on more and more Palestinian territory – massive, organized, indigenous, nonviolent resistance, in fact any resistance, now lacks the energy that was notable during Intifada I and is usually short-lived. The situation now is tragic because it is an historic fact that the first Intifada was succeeding until it was hijacked by the shell game that became the Oslo I and Oslo II "piece" process.

Sis and I experienced evidence of Palestinian weariness and flagging will to resist assertively but nonviolently shortly after our return from this trip (a couple of weeks after the assassination of Sheik Yassin). While shopping one noontime at a busy, commercial intersection in the center of Bethlehem, suddenly shopkeepers began hurriedly and unaccountably to close down. Soon we became aware of a masked Palestinian youth dashing from shop to shop yelling something at the proprietors as he raced by. The merchants immediately began slamming shut the heavy metal doors to their shops.

But not completely.

Each shopkeeper appeared to be peeping furtively out through the still partially open door of his store, intently eyeing the masked youth as he moved down the street. When a store owner asked what was happening, he answered, "We are being told to strike because the Israelis killed someone today." But then the owner did something that took us completely by surprise. As soon as the masked youth disappeared from view, he opened up again – as did shopkeepers on down the complete length of the street. Not a single shop stayed shut.

I had seen that same scenario acted out many times before during Israeli army-imposed curfews in Hebron, but then the refusal to stay shut was in defiance of an occupation-imposed curfew. As soldiers moved down Hebron's main street ordering shops to close, proprietors, especially of grocery stories and bakeries, who seemed to have a sixth sense about how tough the soldiers were going to be about staying closed, watched them progress down the street through a crack in the door and would open up again as soon as the soldiers moved out of sight. Back then, the look on the face of the Hebron shopkeepers was one of glee over the success of their small and certainly spunky act of resistance. But in Bethlehem the look on the face of the shopkeeper to whom we were talking as he opened his shop back up seemed more like embarrassment and perhaps chagrin at being seen by internationals to be putting business before resistance.

Another reason the Israelis know they are winning is because they rarely bother to impose curfews any more; they have figured out that their tight military blockades (called "closures") of the entrances to even the smallest Palestinian hamlets are working just as well, if not better, than the curfews ever did at keeping the lid on. The closures, which still take a lot of soldier power to enforce (but at any given moment take less than curfews do), keep the Palestinians hemmed in and tied down simply by restricting vehicle traffic between villages, towns and cities and then by occasionally launching heavily armed raids into those areas after dark in order to round up alleged terrorists and demolish homes. The result, one discouraged Palestinian activist told me when I visited Nablus in early January, is that "The streets belong to Palestine during the day, but to Israel at night. So sometimes I think it better not to get up."

35

Only Half the Story

Bethlehem, West Bank, Palestine, April 13, 2004

Those who call the barrier going up a "separation" fence are buying into the propaganda of the Israelis and their Israel-right-or-wrong supporters. You can say "separation" if you mean that, as of today, huge portions of the West Bank have been unilaterally "separated" from Palestine. That is hardly what the so-called "peace process" has purportedly been about. As I have said, this is a "piece process" (enabled by the U.S. government) in which piece by piece Palestine is relentlessly being absorbed into a newly emerging "greater" Israel.

From what I gather, even those of us here in the West Bank, back home and elsewhere, who are opposing the "annexation" wall/fence may not completely grasp the success of this cruel unilateral landgrab because international attention on The Wall is focused on what is happening in the northern and central portions of the West Bank. But that is only half the story. Even though there are not miles and miles of serpentine wall to be seen that are laying bare the massive expropriation of Palestinian territory in the south, the same old relentless "annexation" process is under way there, too.

Around Hebron, where there is no wall like the one in the north to be seen, the decades-long campaign of annexation continues—and this process continues to be as dramatically successful as the "annexation" wall/fence is in the north. The main difference is that the insidious fencing in the south gets virtually no attention in the conventional overseas press, not to mention from many governments, including ours in the United States. The response we get from low-level U.S. functionaries, who are the only ones to whom we have access, is essentially, "Your story has touched our hearts, but......"

When we contact stellar American news organizations and suggest they come down to view what we have been seeing, the answer in effect is, "Ho hum." The other day when I offered to show the bureau chief of a major U.S. newsmagazine what is happening around Hebron, he said the last time he was down our way was to do a story about a suicide bomber from the area and he didn't expect to be back until there was another story like that. So the true situation here is virtually unreported. All over the southern half of the West Bank and the environs of Bethlehem and Hebron—most "settlements" large and small, protected by the Israeli army, are engaged in a never-ending process of digging new pathways on Palestinian soil on which new annexation fencing can be installed. That fencing will then extend hundreds of yards deeper into neighboring Palestinian farmlands.

Just after the first of the year the pace quickened for landgrabs in the Ba'qaa Valley and wadis bordering the settlements of Harsina and Kiryat Arba. The settlements, connected by a "settlers-only" road, sit just east of Hebron on top of adjacent hills about a mile apart. In less than a month paths for new annexation fences were far down the hills from both Kiryat Arba and Harsina, quickly cleared by settler earthmoving equipment, all watchfully protected by Israeli soldiers. Soon new fencing sprouted up hundreds of yards further down hill from a previously embedded, less-sophisticated fence systems, which until then had marked the limits of earlier confiscations. In one instance the fences were put in place by student volunteers from a high school in Israel; they had been given time off to journey to the West Bank to help the settlement get the work done as quickly as possible. Another day we encountered Asian laborers doing the same thing.

For the first time a broad corridor of confiscated fields runs along either side of the "settlers-only" connector road. Even while territorial non-contiguity remains a grave issue everywhere for Palestinians, those settlers of Kiryat and Harsina have reached out towards each other and achieved a triumph of contiguity at the expense of Palestinian farmers living in this oppressed corner of the West Bank. Clearly annexation fencing is just as serious for farmers living in the grasping shadow of Kiryat Arba and Harsina as it is for farmers in the north who continue to suffer the same fate. Until late February, CPTers and Palestinians who live and farm between the two settlements could walk east or west through wadis lying between the two settlements. Now they can't.

Recently when I tried to cross the expanding corridor near Kiryat Arba with a group of international fact-finders – something that had been done many times before – we were stopped by armed settler security guards in pickups and Israeli soldiers in three Jeeps. When I told them what I was trying to do, they told us solemnly we couldn't.

"Why? I asked.

"It is dangerous for you," was the answer.

"It never has been before," I said. Naturally I thought they were going to try to convince me that terrorists might attack us, which is the usual line. Instead one soldier said, pointing to an army outpost 100 yards away which I had walked by uneventfully several times in the past, "You see that barracks over there?"

"Yes."

"If you walk by there, the soldiers will shoot you."

"I am not worried about that," I said. "They never have stopped us before."

Then he said firmly we had to vacate the area immediately by walking north via the corridor, which we both knew would take us a few miles out of our way. I finally realized he had been issuing an oblique warning. The rules of the game, he was saying, have changed. It's time to leave the way we tell you to, not the way you want.

Meanwhile, as thousands of acres of Palestinian land continue to be swallowed up that way, the harassment of Palestinians living in the path of these encroachments is also continuing nonstop. Recently several CPTers were called to the home of a friend living several hundred yards down the hill from Harsina, who asked us to help him prune his grapevines. He needed our help because a few days before, settlers had overrun the last of his eight acres of orchards and grape arbors. When the latest extension of the annexation fence had been completed earlier, soldier guards—never settlers—promised our friend and his neighbors they would have access to their land so that they could work it. But Palestinians know that is an old promise the military makes but which it rarely keeps.

After several days of fruitlessly trying to reach a phone number he had been given to obtain permission from the relevant military authority to go through an opening in the fence so he could tend to his remaining grapevines, he called CPT to ask if we would—permission or not—accompany him through the opening in a nonviolent "action," the aim of which would be to get his grapes pruned. Which we did.

Shortly after we filed through the fence and started to prune his vines, first one settler security pickup drove up, then another and then in quick succession three Israeli army Jeeps. Soldiers jumped out and ordered everyone back through the fence. Our friend tried to argue that he had been trying to get permission to prune his grapes by calling the phone number he had been given, but no one answered. Ever!

"Never mind," the soldiers' commander told him and us. "You cannot go there unless you call the number and get permission. There is no other way."

When our friend continued to protest, the soldier threatened to have his house searched. A Palestinian friend who lives in the Old City of Hebron and who had accompanied us to the action tried arguing on our friend's behalf. The commander, much annoyed, took her ID and held it for two hours. He also said that he was going to see that her home was searched too.

Not able to leave the area without her ID, two CPTers rushed back to the Old City to her home to be there with her mother just in case a detachment of soldiers did show up to search it. About 30 minutes after getting there, five Israeli soldiers came tramping into the apartment and conducted a room-by-room scrutiny that this time was carried out without incident except for the outrageous intrusion itself.

Naturally our friend still is not able to get through the fence to tend his grapes. The reason, of course, is because that phone number he was given to call to get the required permission still doesn't answer.

36

Which Came First?

Hebron, West Bank, Palestine, May 23, 2004

Now that the Israeli army has recently been busy in dealing out death and demolition – retail – in Gaza much like it did in Jenin a couple of years ago, comparisons with the remarkably similar U.S. occupation of Iraq are inevitable. Since it is terrifically difficult for CPT to get inside Gaza these days in order to see for ourselves what is happening, I have had to imagine – inspired by videoed news images and reports via Arabic, Western and Israeli news sources as well as the internet – how ominous and menacing the days and nights must be for everyone involved. There are tens of thousands of furious, frightened Palestinians crammed inside the teeming, overcrowded Rafah refugee camp plus seven to eight thousand equally furious, adamantly defiant Israeli settler/squatter/intruders living in Gaza territory, none of whom know whether they or a family member may be the next to be murdered.

On the other side of an ideological divide, these Israelis are determined to remain entrenched atop prime real estate in Gaza – sitting in their ticky-tacky, subsidized dwellings-that-Sharon-built, which now in an about-face he is seriously proposing to abandon. Where the settlers are concerned, it's hard for them these days to tell, from their point of view, the good guys from the bad guys.

(Is there – because of settler outrage – a potentially gruesome similarity between the last days of Itzhak Rabin and the days ahead for Ariel Sharon? Or was the political outlet Sharon gave his followers to express their political will in the form of the Likud party disengagement referendum enough to ensure that – unlike Rabin – whatever happens in the waning months of his government, Ariel Sharon at least will die in bed and not at the hands of a fellow Israeli?)

The terrible repression going on in Gaza – especially for the Palestinians – with its rising tide of blood and home demolitions reminds me of the made-in-the-U.S.A. nouveau-hell that of late has been imposed on Iraq. With attention in the U.S. fixed on the escalating carnage mutually perpetrated and perpetuated by the persistent Iraqi armed resistance to the U.S.-inspired occupation of Iraq by the diminishing Coalition of the Willing, I began to describe the occupation butchery and incarcerations in Iraq as "Gaza East." But then those recent stories concerning the tortures and even murders that reportedly took place inside a U.S. military prison in Baghdad and elsewhere got me thinking that I had it backwards and that all along I should have been calling Gaza "Iraq West." For a bit last week it seemed I had been right the first time: the Israeli army's currently murderous destructive Rafah operation made the U.S. violence in Iraq seem to be – relatively speaking – a reflection of what Israel has been doing for years in Gaza. So I'm back to referring to Iraq as "Gaza East." But then came the killing-field atrocity in northern Iraq where a wedding party was decimated by our occupation forces. So now, which is it?

With U.S. and Israeli practices so remarkably and transparently similar, some assessors have begun looking back in order to figure out who first learned what from whom and when. Which came first – the chicken or the egg? For a while we have heard the claim that Israel's military played a mentoring role to the U.S. in dealing with urban resistance. Stories still circulate that prior to the invasion of Iraq the U.S. sent special forces personnel to observe first-hand the way the Israeli army handled the Palestinian uprising in and around Jenin. But I think this is forgetting the folks who brought you My Lai in 1968, the School of the Americas, Guantanamo Bay and also others who disingenuously included the Al Jazeera bureaus in Kabul and Baghdad on the list of the very first sites to be targeted for destruction. It also denigrates the U.S. military's professional ability for grim originality and sadistic expertise when it comes to torture and other forms of prisoner abuse. Perhaps Jenin and other killing venues during the second uprising in the West Bank can be called Israeli refresher course rather than an actual tutoring of innovative techniques in violent mass repression and suppression.

Meanwhile Palestinian reaction to the Iraq torture stories has been consistently different from the how-can-this-be-astonishment of so many Americans – because where most Palestinian male adults, older youth and too many Palestinian women are concerned, when it comes to being on the receiving end of arbitrary detentions and cruel and inhumane treatment in prisons run by some democracies, they've been there and done that. Detention without charges and the niceties of due process, which are supposed to prevent extrajudicial torture and lesser punishments, is the name of the game in the current holier-than-thou, post-totalitarian environment in which we now are obliged to live, all the outcome of a radicalized Israel and the radical American right. The Palestinians have been sensitive to this awful truth for a long time.

This "old as the hills" condition ignores boundaries of conscience long ago set by internationally agreed-to conventions about occupation and incarceration practices. Instead, today all seem hellbent on systematically eliminating restraints on coercive violence. That is why Palestinians scoff bitterly when they hear or read about Israelis who describe their army as the "most moral in the world." Palestinians are also among the first to point sadly to an immoral (or at least amoral) equivalent to that description, which has been revived in the U.S. to describe its military: the old canard that portrays U.S. men and women involved in the ongoing occupation of Iraq as "freedom fighters."

When it comes to assessing the use and abuse of military coercion by both Israel and the United States, it really doesn't matter which comes first, the chicken or the egg, when both the chicken and the egg are diseased and rotten.

37

"Piece Process" Update

Hebron, West Bank, Palestine, May 25, 2004

A section of the "annexation" wall has reached the western edge of Qalandiya checkpoint, south of Ramallah. This bars West Bank Palestinians coming down from the north from entering Jerusalem. It was positioned – of course unilaterally – a considerable distance inside the Palestine side of the checkpoint, a quarter mile from where IDs and passports are currently checked. This barrier is similar to the one in East Jerusalem that drastically slices through Abu Dis and puts Al-Quds University on the "wrong" side of the West Bank from most of its student body and faculty. Unfortunately, this section of the wall has become the site of several shootings of distressed Palestinians trying to get from one side to the other.

South of Jerusalem, a similar unilateral scenario is unfolding where the wall has wormed its way up a hill northeast of Bethlehem to the eastern edge of the defunct Hebron Road that traverses the Tantur checkpoint separating Jerusalem from Bethlehem. Once the main thoroughfare south from Jerusalem through Bethlehem to Hebron, now the Hebron Road is abruptly blocked a half-mile down from the Tantur checkpoint by a forbidding Israeli army stockade that encloses and seals off the heavily guarded Rachel's

Tomb locale from the rest of Bethlehem. And thus another religious site is lost to the West Bank as a tourist attraction.

As at Qalandiya, the "annexation" wall at Tantur has been positioned a considerable distance *inside* the Palestinian (Bethlehem) side of the checkpoint, about 400 yards away from where IDs and passports are currently checked. Each day those who must pass there can witness the relentless construction of a huge terminus being built against the wall that covers a quarter square mile of former Palestinian fields, orchards and homes. Gun-toting private security guards, hired to protect the construction going on inside the still-open-to-view enclosure, keep the curious from looking around – and especially from taking pictures.

You can still see inside well enough to get an idea about what is planned for this increasingly constricted corner of the West Bank. Materializing before the eyes of the dispossessed is an immense, super-fortified complex for the paranoid. Apparently the Israeli army hopes it will give them a vast protected space – similar to the Eretz crossing at Gaza – in which its almost omnipotent bureaucracy will be able to regulate forcefully and in minute detail or, when they choose, completely choke off the flow of Palestinians and their goods that need to be moved in or out and through the increasingly fractionated West Bank.

A West Bank Palestinian needing to go to Jerusalem without any enabling documents, such as a note from a doctor confirming a medical appointment, cannot be assured of passage through a checkpoint. That decision is left up to an often-bored, angry or simply downright mean young Israeli soldier or border police on duty at the time. The uncertainty due to caprice forces literally thousands of Palestinians every day to attempt getting in and out of Jerusalem by riskier means. A Palestinian passing through the Tantur or Qalandiya checkpoint who hasn't been delayed too long may be able to get to the Damascus Gate at the heart of East Jerusalem in 30 or 40 more minutes. Trying to avoid the checkpoint, sneaking in or out through bumpy side roads and around checkpoints may take as long as two or three hours. If the Palestinian is subsequently collared on a Jerusalem street at an impromptu police or army checkpoint, the person may risk imprisonment, certainly an uncomfortably large fine, or if a male, a clandestine beating out of sight of potentially interfering eyes.

Meanwhile further south in Hebron, the Israeli confiscation noose continues to tighten in much the same way. The pace of the "annexation" wall which is choking off farming areas outside the city in the vicinity of Kiryat Arba and Harsina settlements is also affecting the hapless Palestinian inhabitants frantically trying to hang on and survive in Hebron's Old City. Along the perimeter of the city the Israeli army barriers and checkpoints are severely restricting access to fields and homes.

Most of the entrances leading to the Old City, formerly blocked with loosely strung barbed wire barriers, flimsy screening or temporary-looking guard structures, are now sealed off by solid metal dividers, rigid fences and increasingly elaborate bullet-proof guardhouses. Thus at the Beit Romano checkpoint at the north end of the Old City, in the past couple of weeks the relatively vulnerable camouflage-netting-covered guardhouse is gone. It has been replaced with a thick-walled, circular cement guardhouse with bulletproof, slit-like windows all around.

After installing this, an equally high barrier of thick cement slabs was set in place – an imposing, solid barrier which extends some ten feet from one side of the street to the guardhouse – making the structure jut so far into the street there is only a narrow opening left, just wide enough for a single vehicle to pass through at a time. This week, across a small plaza from the guardhouse, Israeli soldiers positioned a heavy cement roadblock across the already narrow entrance to the Old City that slows down foot traffic emerging into the plaza and approaching the checkpoint.

Since late April this refortified Beit Romano checkpoint has been the site of an unprecedented campaign of Israeli army harassment. Until then, Israeli guards detained mostly young men, but now senior citizens and even boys in short pants are also being stopped. Besides having their IDs checked, many are ordered to lift their shirts to their shoulders so the soldiers can see if they are concealing anything. "This is how we catch terrorists," is the explanation they give. Palestinian boys and men who object are often ordered to turn around and stand spread-eagled against the wall while an angry soldier prods or punches him in the back to stand up straighter.

Now the military are routinely stopping women as well, ordering them, like the men and boys, to stand against a wall while their IDs are checked. Many are told to open their purses and shopping bags so they can be searched, while others, usually the younger ones, are ordered out of sight into the guardhouse for a more intimate frisking by female soldiers. Even children are being routinely stopped these days and the contents of their school bags or backpacks searched.

Israeli soldiers stationed around the Old City have been stepping up their patrols within the city too, so several times throughout the day or night they move from the Beit Romano checkpoint at one end to the Ibrahimi Mosque special security zone at the other, stopping to prod baskets and boxes of produce deeply and search other wares for concealed weapons. They wave metal detecting wands over bags of bread, neatly arranged mounds or bulging baskets of fresh vegetables and fruit, as well as other items on display outside the handful of shops still fitfully open for business. The soldiers also stop the small tractors hauling compact wagons in the narrow passageways of the Old City, vendors and their pushcarts and even boys pulling wagons in order to poke the contents thoroughly before letting them proceed. Other times they randomly stop and set up a flying checkpoint to institute a surprise ID check hoping to flush out someone on the Israeli security apparatus' "wanted" list.

38

While You Were Gone
Episode 3

Hebron, West Bank, Palestine, November 16, 2004

Each time we leave Palestine and Israel, we worry about what will happen while we are gone. This time when we left Palestine in early June the two-story-high color photomural of Yassir Arafat which had been removed the year before from its place of prominence above the entrance to Hebron's municipal building was still down. (Hebron is Hamas country.) As soon as it was evident that he was mortally ill, the sign suddenly reappeared the week before last. "He is our national symbol of resistance," more than one Hebron resident, critics all of Arafat's domestic administration, said "and for that we honor him."

Following the before-dawn confirming announcement of his death, and as daylight began to replace the darkness, the most militant acknowledgment of this event was the plumes of black smoke from burning tires. They had been placed every 100 yards along the main road heading north up from Bab iZaweyya to Halhoul three miles away. At midmorning, stores which had opened briefly, began closing out of deference to his memory without any prompting by the Israeli army.

Soldiers and border police, however, had already beefed up their presence at checkpoints leading in and out of the Old City, and a patrol of four soldiers in a Jeep did sally forth briefly into Bab iZaweyya, where they shot a tear-gas canister towards a small group of Palestinian bystanders clustered kitty-corner to them across the main intersection. After several wary minutes during which the groups, still at a distance, eyed each other cautiously, one of the soldiers yelled out, "If anyone throws a stone, we will make a really tight curfew!" Some of the Palestinians rolled their eyes as if to say, "We know he doesn't mean it," and soon the soldier and his three comrades got in the Jeep and drove back towards H2.

The soldier's threat notwithstanding, curfews, tight or otherwise, are mostly a form of collective punishment rarely employed by the Israeli army these days. Closures – selective or complete – which are both restrictive and punishing, have taken the place of curfews. They have become the favored way for keeping the lid on, because they require fewer troops and as a result are comparatively cost-effective in terms of potential jeopardy and funds expended. It appears that the army's tacticians decided that putting a lot of troops in harm's way by sending them into Palestinian villages, towns and cities to patrol streets in order to insure that shops are closed and everyone is humiliated by being shut up at home wasn't worth it. Why go to all that dangerous effort, when simply not letting anyone leave or enter town will do just as well?

It is claimed that a complete closure of the entire West Bank can be accomplished in less than five minutes. I can believe it. Since the reoccupation began over two years ago, Israeli soldiers and border police have been strategically positioned in and around many villages, towns and cities so they can be quickly dispatched to implement closure at the more than 700 checkpoints, partial checkpoints, roadblocks, heavy-metal road gates, earth mounds, earth walls, trenches and a rising number of olive-drab cylindrical observation towers. This means that now the entire West Bank can be sealed off as effectively as can Gaza. The count of blockages around Hebron is by far the highest—206 according to a count taken last summer, with Nablus next at 114, Ramallah at 98 and Bethlehem at 96.

Despite the closures, a few thousand Palestinians were permitted to go to Ramallah for Arafat's funeral; others made their way in riskily and clandestinely. Tens of thousands who wanted to be there, were blocked by the total "lock down" of the West Bank. At midmorning I was on my way to Bethlehem in a jitney that was waved back into Hebron when it tried to enter Highway 60, the main north-south bypass highway from the Galilee through the West Bank into the Negev. This meant a trip that recently had taken me an hour and a half to complete nonstop took us three hours with enforced stops along the way. Our driver took his Palestinian passengers and me to a high earth barricade at the north end of Halhoul where we climbed over to the other side and caught another jitney whose driver had sneaked onto Highway 60 over back roads hoping he might make it to Bethlehem. He didn't.

First he was turned back at a floating (impromptu) checkpoint at the Gush Etzion interchange, two-thirds of the way between Hebron and Bethlehem. Out of sight of the soldiers at the checkpoint, he circumvented the interchange over more back roads and reëntered Highway 60, a mile further on and sped off toward Bethlehem. But an army Jeep came tearing up the highway from behind and drew alongside, motioning the driver to pull over. He did. The Jeep darted by and stopped in front. Two soldiers jumped out and standing in front of the jitney pointed their guns at us. Another soldier examined everyone's IDs. The driver and his Palestinian passengers were ordered to turn around and head back. The soldier said to me, "You're an American. Go!" So I went—walking the last mile into Bethlehem while the jitney headed off slowly in the other direction.

Some may think that closures signify a retreat by the Israeli army from one of its more onerous forms of collective punishment—the curfews. The truth is, however, it's not an indication of some kind of backing away, but instead a sign of the awful fact that Israel (enabled by the U.S. government) is winning and knows that its appalling campaign to diminish Palestinian territory and exhaust and subdue its hapless, oppressed and suppressed people is succeeding.

For example: while attention—such as it is—remains focused on the ongoing construction of the "annexation" wall (the most extreme form of closure) in the north and around Jerusalem, bulldozers recently began preparing for it in the south. A few miles west of Hebron, a path for the barrier is being carved out (with U.S. blessing) atop a ridge several hundred meters inside the West Bank. Because of that imminent land theft, dozens of West Bank Palestinian olives tree will be located out of reach in Israel.

39

Remembrance of Horrors Past and Present
Iraq 2004/Lebanon 1984

Hebron, West Bank, Palestine, November 20, 2004

I usually don't write about places where I am not, but in this report I need to write about a place where I have been but am not now – because Margaret Hassan is dead.

To begin at the beginning, where inhuman behavior is concerned, a grisly Newton's Third Law ("For every action there is an equal and opposite reaction") applies, but it doesn't work out quite as neatly here as it did in physics class. Margaret Hassan died because when meanness, cruelty, viciousness, brutality and all forms of violent abuse are concentrated, then a logical, rational, inanimate symmetrical equivalence is replaced by an invariably less exact and terribly frightening animate asymmetry. So Margaret died because of the foreseeable, out-of-control, escalating nature of Newton's dangerously volatile Third Law of inhuman behavior – exemplified by self-proclaimed good guys bent on not just forestalling but also retaliating against those they designate as bad. But the more violent the issue, the more desperate the struggle, the more so-called good guys run into a serious problem – they can't put their hands on a single "enemy," So they take out "friends" instead.

Margaret Hassan is also dead because bad guys who insist they are good guys never own up to the fact that in existential terms they might not be nearly as good as they insist they are. These days Western triumphalists and triumphant Westerners see the struggle for Iraq (and also for Palestine, by the way) as an efficacious and virtuous clash between democracy and theological/political fundamentalism or – as it came to be described 20 years ago – a conflict between "the evil empire" and "the great Satan." This lack of consistent equilibrium where violent human behavior is concerned makes "tit for tat" seem like the good old days. Even such a primitive behavioral concept as "eye for an eye" is continuing to escalate in Iraq (and Palestine and Israel) to seventy times seven eyes for one – and worse.

Sis and I met Margaret Hassan only briefly in Baghdad during the chaotic six weeks following the fall of the city. She was in charge of CARE's large and internationally respected relief operations, and we were members of CPT's small team. But both groups were part of the remnant of humanitarian organizations still trying to operate in Baghdad. Most week days we made our way to Saddam Hussein's former administrative compound for occupation updates delivered by mid-level American and British officers. Our hope was that these "professionals" would "finally" report satisfactory progress in the Allies' efforts to rebuild infrastructure.

But never was heard the "finally" word. Instead – nonstop – we heard discouraging words, often in the form of accusations and pronouncements. They declared that it was the responsibility of the handful of NGOs and other humanitarian groups like CPT to initiate the rebuilding process, not the military's. But Margaret Hassan, standing up to such indecent evasions of moral responsibility, repeatedly took the lead in telling truth to the coalition's power. Those mid-level martial marionettes, with the straightest of faces, never wavered from their stubbornly defended position despite preinvasion warnings by every official and unofficial specialist worth their training and intellectual integrity. The gist of those warnings was that the "mission" against Iraq, no matter how it was being publicly proclaimed from one day to the next, could not be "accomplished" if simply investing the region with soldiers was the military's objective.

But actions, of course, do speak more loudly than words, so where jump-starting reconstruction efforts was concerned, it quickly became clear to us at those briefings that we were dealing with a coalition of the unwilling. Although we were assured that security was the military's concern, we soon figured out that security meant one thing to our briefing officers and to us – and the Iraqis – security meant something much stronger and "fairer." Confidence-building measures, like moving quickly to restore essential energy, healthcare, sustenance and civil-protection services, would have demonstrated palpable concerns for the so-called "liberated." But positive measures were neglected in favor of an occupation that immediately began to acquire the characteristics of Israel's occupation of Gaza and the West Bank.

Instead of trying to win over the populace, the military's main concern seemed to be sticking to the Bush administration's game plan: rebuilding privatized infrastructure. It soon was clear the policy underlying that process had far more to do with proving the efficacy of globalizing – corporatizing, actually – the pursuit of plutocratic-happiness rather than providing Iraqis with the means to acquire the four freedoms, especially the ones relating to freedom "from want" and "from fear."

So Margaret Hassan was kidnapped and murdered: in part – the case needs to be made – an innocent victim of the coalition's morally deficient leadership that was either scandalously shortsighted or deceitfully premeditated. This does not absolve her brutally militant killers from trying to portray her death as something other than what it clearly was: a hideous, cynical, cold-blooded murder. On the face of it, one would think she would have been the last person her violent insurgent captors, who were and are trying to coerce the invaders into withdrawing from Iraq, would think of harming. In love with her Iraqi husband, in love with the

Iraqi people, in love with their faith, for 30 years she had worked tirelessly to address her people's gravest needs tangibly.

Since she was no one's enemy, why was she murdered? I pondered the why's of such questions when I found myself in similar straits 20 years ago as a hostage in Lebanon. Like Margaret Hassan, I was not an enemy and neither were most of the other Western hostages taken then – and our captors knew it. My conclusion then was that in desperate, uneven violent conflicts there are no friends or enemies – just warm bodies, pawns which either side uses cruelly to make their point. The tragedy of Margaret Hassan and all the others is that 20 years ago the level of U.S. military involvement on the ground, in the air and on the high seas in Lebanon was tiny compared to the massive level of involvement and ferocity shown in Iraq today. So the retaliatory level of the resistance back then, with respect to noncombatants, was considerably less ferocious. Now in Iraq the peril to noncombatants has risen in direct proportion to the exponential increase in the number of occupying troops, their ferocity and the determination of both sides to make their points.

So what can I conclude from the murder of Margaret Hassan? Perhaps a reworking of an old truism applies: The more things stay the same the more they are destined to change.

But not existentially for the better.

40

CTSD!

Hebron, West Bank, Palestine, December 4, 2004

It's been a while since the term PTSD (Post Traumatic Stress Disorder) became a commonplace. Where traumatic stresses and the disorders resulting from them are concerned, I think there is a condition worse than PTSD. It's called Chronic Traumatic Stress Disorder (CTSD): the scarring and re-scarring of a person by violence that never stops. Victims never reach the point where relentless ongoing stress – deliberately applied – can be left behind. Therefore, they cannot move into a "post traumatic" phase where presumably there is a better chance for recovery and healing.

To exemplify what I mean about CTSD, I am going to tell you about the beleaguered, careworn adults and children of At-Tuwani who, in the face of unrelenting, too often violent domination, struggle from one day to the next to hang on to their way of life and a surviving dignity which they amazingly still are able to muster. At-Tuwani is a small, ancient Palestinian village situated too close for comfort to Ma'on, one of the militant, violently acquisitive Israeli settlements in the Yatta hills southeast of Hebron.

Ma'on was suddenly established in 1982 on a nearby hilltop by Israeli squatters. From that day to this the people of At-Tuwani have been the victims of continuous physical intimidation and the unrelenting theft of their agricultural holdings: acreage made rich over hundreds of years of patient labor by the local farmers who diligently carved their plots out of the rocky soil surrounding the village. More than a generation of repression, suppression and oppression against the people of the village has been carried out by smirking, swaggering, often-snarling Settlers who know they can count on, if not the connivance of the Israeli army stationed in the area, at least its passive acquiescence.

I first wrote about the gradual reduction of At-Tuwani in chapter two above. Confiscation of At-Tuwani land began some two years after Ma'on was established less than a mile away from the village. The area where we stood during the encounter described in my second report, along with its acre or so of olive trees, has long since been confiscated. The ring of confiscated land around the settlement continues to expand some 20 to 25 acres a year. That may not seem like much to an American or Canadian, but for the village's five families with some 150 to 200 members, the total amount of cultivatable soil now lost to them because it is out of their reach behind settlement fences adds up to about 375 acres.

In Palestine that's a lot. And, by the way, earlier this year, settlers poisoned one of the village's two drinking water wells by throwing dead chickens into it.

Unremunerated confiscation of their property, however, is just one dingy facet of the villagers' continuing peril and travail. Besides their land thefts, settlers 20 years ago began a relentless campaign of physical attacks on the villagers (including children) ranging from beatings to deliberate, closeup shootings. The "including children" is what brought CPT back to At-Tuwani, more or less to stay, in September. Some four years ago, settlers began a stepped-up campaign of not only menacing but actually attacking youngsters from a nearby village as they walked to and from the area's primary school in At-Tuwani. The shortest route for the schoolchildren (two kilometers) is a rocky hilly road that skirts the settlement. The hilliness is significant, because settlers hiding in nearby trees would wait there undetected until the kids got close enough that it was difficult for them to dash to safety.

This year only five pupils are braving the settlers' terrifying daily gauntlet, but when school began in September, the situation was so bad for them that CPT and Italian partners from a similar faith-based, nonviolent organization, Operation Dove, were asked to establish a constant presence in the village. The internationals subsequently began escorting the five children as they walked fearfully back and forth to school. This displeased the settlers of Ma'on, to say the least. Not long after the accompaniments began, two CPTers were rushed to a hospital after being attacked by settler youths dressed in black, their faces hidden by black scarves. Dashing from their tree cover, swinging bats and chains, the settlement thugs were not quick enough to reach the fleeing children, but they did catch up to the internationals who stood between them and the attackers.

The young black shirts, who could well have been some of the same mooning brats I described back in 2002, but now were older, bigger, stronger and more frighteningly brazen, had plenty of time to flail and beat the CPTers to the ground. Police and soldiers stationed nearby nevertheless took 30 minutes to arrive on scene in answer to CPT's immediate calls for help, giving the settlement's proto-Ku Kluxers sufficient time to break one CPTer's arm and bruise her knee badly, while the other CPTer's lung was punctured when his ribs were broken. (After stays in hospitals both returned to their work in At-Tuwani and elsewhere in the West Bank.) That dangerous episode, however, was not the end of serious injuries. A few days later another CPTer and an Amnesty International observer were battered by more bat, chain and slingshot wielding masked bullies. An Operation Dove accompanier was injured so severely in the attack, he still has not recovered fully. Happily, no child has been hurt since the accompaniments began.

Partly as a result of complaints and inquiries filed with Israel from around the world, Israeli military occupation authorities agreed to provide a police or military escort for the children during their frightening walk to and from school – but not along the short route skirting the settlement. They must go another way, several kilometers longer, with the proviso that the army or the police do the accompanying, not CPT, Operation Dove or other internationals. Team members are still stationed in At-Tuwani, however, and – among several tasks – they daily monitor (from a hilltop 400 yards away) the slow progress on foot of those five kids and their military escort (riding securely in an Israeli army Jeep and an Israeli police vehicle) to and from school. Their anxiety remains because settler toughs often come down from their trees to line the route in order to frighten the kids (or worse) while their Israeli armed escort, sometimes slow to react, leads its charges diffidently onward.

CTSD!

41

CTSD!
Part 2

Hebron, West Bank, Palestine, December 12, 2004

Hassan (not his real name, although he is very real) spends quite a bit of time looking out for CPT and Operation Dove's needs and comfort, since members of each have been living in his village of At-Tuwani. He belongs to this tiny Palestinian agricultural community situated in the south Hebron hills and he has suffered long from the marauding, mauling attacks of the violently militant residents of the nearby Israeli settlement of Ma'on. It was Hassan who – on behalf of the villagers – worriedly contacted CPT and Operation Dove in September, asking the two organizations to accompany the five children who daily walk to school from the nearby village of Tuba.

It became painfully evident that Hassan had not exaggerated the severity of the problem when, shortly after the accompaniments began, masked bat- and chain-wielding settler youths made no distinction between the children's international protectors and the children themselves. The resulting injuries to the internationals and lingering physical and emotional distress in the wake of the attacks has served to exemplify personally the CTSD that afflicts Palestinians literally nonstop. This is true not just in At-Tuwani but everywhere in the West Bank and Gaza because of the unending, relentless, damaging nature of the occupation.

The other day Hassan mentioned that parents of twelve other primary school children from Tuba (who had been pulled out of the At-Tuwani school after the stepped-up settler menace began in September) were beginning to think of allowing their kids to return to At-Tuwani next semester. But because of their fear of more attacks, the parents had chosen to send them on a two-hour walk each way to a school serving Bedouin communities a few miles south of At-Tuwani – the longer route being relatively "safer" than the much shorter one to At-Tuwani. Now, Hassan said, the parents were daring to hope that the daily Israeli military and police escort of the primary school youngsters might make a difference. Those Tuba parents were hoping the settlers would stop attacking the children now that they had Israeli police protecting them.

No such luck.

The very next morning a CPTer and an Operation Dove volunteer took their customary positions on a ridge overlooking the route of the small procession from Tuba. They soon realized the next few minutes were not going to be trouble free. Some ten minutes before an Israeli army Jeep, followed closely by the walking children and then a police car, were expected to appear at the top of the hill, a few youthful voices, hidden from view on the other side could be heard singing loudly in Hebrew a robust Israeli marching song. It was hard to tell how many were gathered out of sight, but it seemed pretty certain they were near the route the children would be following. The path runs along the edge of an evergreen forest covering the Ma'on settlement outpost of Havot Ma'on – a perfect hiding place for settlement bullies.

After a few minutes the raucous singing stopped and the area became eerily silent. The noise of the bratty ensemble had even silenced the birds that had been chirping sweetly away before the unseen boys, who seemed to be pumping themselves up emotionally, began their intrusive singing.

After the time had passed when the procession was expected to come into view, the Operation Dove observer clutched a pair of binoculars and kept anxiously watching the spot where they were expected. Another five minutes passed and still no procession. The silence now seemed ominous. Suddenly a dog on the far side of the hill began barking excitedly, then another and another. The trio of angry dogs kept up their yelping for another minute. Then again silence.

At last an Israeli army Jeep, moving uncharacteristically fast, appeared over the lip of the hill and scurried down the near side followed by the police Jeep stirring up a cloud of dust as they moved briskly past the thickly forested edge of the outpost. No children were seen. Suddenly there was a loud crash as something hit one of the vehicles on the side facing the trees. Silence descended as the vehicles drove out of hearing distance. They kept moving swiftly along the bumpy road toward the site at At-Tuwani where they end their run each morning. The CPT and Operation Dove observers hoped that the children – all safe – would be in one of the vehicles, but they could only wait and watch as the procession rolled on for six more minutes.

Finally the vehicles stopped at the drop-off point and all five children got out of the police vehicle and headed off to school. "That figures," the Operation Dove observers said, assuming that some incident had taken place on the other side of the hill. "The army never does anything to stop the settlers when they make trouble. The police, if they decide to help, are the ones who must do it."

Rightly or wrongly, the reason for his conclusion is that Israeli soldiers are not allowed to lay a hand on recalcitrant settlers, while Israeli police can and sometimes do. Also after the attacks on the CPT and Operation Dove escorts, one of the left-leaning Israeli newspapers ran a story to the effect that the army admitted it might have gone too far at times in its deference to settlement leadership and that mid-level army officers in the West Bank had been taking orders from settlement security coördinators. The article also mentioned that many army officers live in some of the most virulent settlements. There seems to be a question as to who runs the occupied territories – the army or the settlers – and the activities were getting out of the army's control.

As soon as the children were seen walking safely from the drop-off point to the school, the CPT and Operation Dove observers went to get the story. The children explained that as the procession approached the last hill before At-Tuwani which runs along the tree-lined edge of the outpost, they could see a vehicle belonging to the settlement school parked there with a woman waiting inside the cab. Suddenly two students brandishing thick wooden staffs came rushing out of the trees at the kids. By the time the army Jeep came to a stop, the settlement toughs were within 40 yards of the frightened youngsters. A police officer jumped out of his vehicle and hurriedly herded them into it. Then they tore off over the top of the hill into view of the observers. A student said that the crashing sound the observers had heard was one of four or five rocks that had been thrown at the police by settlers hidden in the trees.

Discussing the incident later, Hassan said a village leader had called the local occupation administrator to complain. "Don't worry," the administrator told the leader. "We will solve the problem." Hassan snickered at that assurance.

"What about those parents in Tuba who are thinking of letting their children go back to school in At-Tuwani next semester," Hassan was asked. "Will they still take the chance?

"Only if they can get 17 in the police car," was his reply.

It's important to comprehend that At-Tuwani is not atypical of Palestine. What has been, is and will be happening to At-Tuwani's and Tuba's beleaguered, careworn families and those in the Bedouin communities a few miles to the south is a story that has been, is and, you can be sure, will continue to take place in and around every West Bank village, town, and city.

CTSD!

42

CTSD!
Part 3

Hebron, West Bank, Palestine, December 15, 2004

Chronic Traumatic Stress Disorder (CTSD) exists when there is no end or respite to the expectation of additional debilitating stress at any moment: no appreciable space in which CTSD has a chance to at least become PTSD (Post Traumatic Stress Disorder). This debilitating problem persists throughout Palestine.

When our friend Hassan first asked CPT and Operation Dove to establish an ongoing presence there, he was hoping their presence would discourage the stepped-up efforts by squatters living in the adjacent Ma'on settlement to prevent villagers from bettering their meager living conditions. All this time Ma'on's sneaky and violent vandals, with the protection of Labor- and Likud-led Israeli governments, have continued to improve their own living conditions. What enraged these intrusive settlers was that the people of At-Tuwani had the nerve to want to build a clinic! And they are actually doing this without official written permission. The slowly rising structure could be demolished at any time, just as, back in 1987, their brand new mosque was destroyed because it had been built without a permit.

The parents of Hassan originally were not from At-Tuwani and he told us that only once had he gone to see the place where his mother and father, their parents and others in their extended families had lived for generations as self-sufficient farmers. Several years ago when his parents were still alive he accompanied them on their first journey back since running away from their birth-place – running for their lives one nightmarish day in 1948. In the tumultuous months after Israel declared itself an exclusivist Jewish state, it began conducting a kind of modern-day Punic War. The goal was not only to defend itself from several Arab nations but also to preëmptively destroy as much Palestinian presence and identity as possible. This aspect of Israel's struggle had little to do with security – it was all about conquest (wolfish colonial expansion in defensive sheep's clothing). Malign colonization rather than benign emigration has been modern Zionism's elephant in the room ever since Theodor Herzl created the political concept over a century ago.

This assessment of revisionist Israeli historical scholarship and research flies in the face of decades-long official Israeli doublethink, double-talk and Newspeak. At one time I applauded Israeli historian Benny Morris because of his research which irrefutably exposed Israel's longstanding ethnic cleansing of and confiscatory designs on the West Bank. But my admiration waned when I read an interview in *Haaretz* earlier this year in which Morris condemned, not the brutal expulsions he had verified, but instead complained that Israel's leaders made a monumental blunder in not completing the job of forcing all Palestinians from their homes, off their land and out of the region when Israel theoretically had a chance to do all that in 1948.

The favorite euphemism of "Land of Israel" radicals for this kind of expulsion is "transfer." They removed more than 400 historic Palestinian villages on the Israeli side of the armistice line and they "transferred" close to a million Palestinians into Gaza, the West Bank and beyond. The village in which Hassan's parents were born and lived was one of the 400, and his family was one of those forced to move on. The site is just a handful of miles south of At-Tuwani on the Israeli side of the armistice line. After the 1967 war that boundary became the so-called Green Line which until recently outlined the border between the West Bank and Israel.

Of course, that border is now fast becoming an irrelevant, nonexistent line on a map because the "annexation" wall/fence is inexorably being built well *inside* the Green Line. When finished, that wall will leave for Palestinians less than half of the West Bank and put the more than half of it that Israel is stealing on the other side inside Israel. When completed, Israel will have created history's largest ghetto. The West Bank land being grabbed and folded into Israel by the wall is a fruit of "unilateralism," the long-time Ariel Sharon strategy that swiftly bloomed when George Bush and his cronies adapted the Sharon "unilateralism" model to their own needs. (Déjà vu: Fallujah is Sabra and Shatila all over again.)

The extraordinary territorial gains that Sharon has made by simply taking without negotiation (and with U.S. blessing) are the kind that such two-faced Labor leaders as Itzhak Rabin in the past and Peres and Barak today could only dream about but never achieve. For this reason neither Peres nor Barak is repudiating the overall aim of Sharon's retreat from Gaza. His goal is to create a geopolitical climate in which Israel can finesse colonizing the areas of the West Bank. For decades Israel has considered this its ideological, political, defensive and environmental bottom line except for four small villages in the north. Gazan land has always been expendable to Israel's radical and real-politic-oriented establishment but not to Israel's radical much-more-ideological establishment.

When Hassan, his parents and siblings got to the village site, he recalls, his mother suddenly began to wail and cry bitterly. The village, of course they knew before arriving, would not be there – only the ruins of the simple stone dwellings and blocked-up caves which had been home to so many could still be seen. However, even though such a sight was expected, it was a harsh reminder to his mother of that day – long before Hassan and siblings were born

–when a large contingent of mechanized Israeli soldiers suddenly appeared and began shooting.

More than 40 years ago it had been a happy prosperous village with about 200 sheep in each of the flocks belonging to the various families and with rich land around the village for grazing. (Sheep in the flocks these days around At-Tuwani number no more than 20.) On entering the village, the soldiers had killed the sheep as well as village shepherds on duty in the fields–two of whom were brothers of Hassan's father–uncles he would never know. Once amongst the houses and caves where the villagers lived, the Israelis gunned down other residents who had not fled fast enough after hearing shots and seeing soldiers firing their guns. The dead from long ago included another uncle Hassan would never know. There was no time to take much of anything with them. The people headed north out of what clearly was going to be Israeli territory from now on and into what, by the war's end, became Jordan's West Bank. After several hours, the families of Hassan's future parents stopped and settled in At-Tuwani.

Ethnic as well as religious survival has never been as certain in At-Tuwani since Israel wrested control of the Hebron hills from Jordan in 1967. The downhill course of hopes and expectations took another turn for the worse in 1980 when an ultranationalist group from Israel showed up one day and started planting trees on top of a hill one rise over from At-Tuwani. Now 24 years later a tall, thick evergreen forest shrouds what became Havat Ma'on, an outpost of the settlement of Ma'on which was established two years later one hilltop over from At-Tuwani. Havat Ma'on provides perfect cover for Settlement bullies who perpetually swoop down to prey on and menace the villagers.

Now a second generation of "settler brats" is following in the meanspirited footsteps of their parents–attacking defenseless shepherds, small children on their way to school, even the pregnant and the elderly. They uproot olive trees, prevent village farmers from cultivating and harvesting their crops or else burn the crops. They have followed up these outrageous harassments by putting fences around fields and orchards, stealing them outright in order to cheekily and sneeringly retain them for their own use and profit. At night, and even sometimes during the day, settlers form vigilante posses that descend on outlying houses to stone and shoot at windows in order to frighten families into leaving.

Such scare tactics worked at two other villages closer to Ma'on than is At-Tuwani. In 1997 the frightened residents of Kharruba and Serora, after 15 years of constant and often-violent pressure, finally abandoned their homes and their longstanding way of life. A law on the Israeli books allows the state to confiscate agricultural land that has not been worked for three years, so recently, settlers from Ma'on began plowing some of Kharruba's abandoned fields.

Nothing infuriates a militant, acquisitive Zionist more quickly than to 1) claim that criticism of the manner in which Israel has pursued the occupation of the West Bank and Gaza is *not* anti-Semitic, or 2) that what has been happening in the occupied territories is a contemporary holocaust. (The holocaust claim tends to boil down to how many dead Palestinians compared to dead Jews does it take to make a holocaust.) To get involved in a numbers game dishonors the memories of Jews and Palestinians alike.

However, I do know a pogrom when I see one. CTSD!

43

Seasons Greetings

Bethlehem, West Bank, Palestine, December 19, 2004

It has been 20 years since I spent Christmas as a hostage, locked away in a hidden room on a mountainside overlooking Lebanon's Beqaa Valley. So I want to mark that anniversary by recalling some of those moments because they were my first as a person of faith. (They are part of a longer remembrance first published in a booklet, "Recollections of My First Noel.")

That Christmas Eve in 1984 I heard footsteps in the hall outside my dark, crypt-like room. The sound was the signal to pull my blindfold down over my eyes. I heard the click of a latch, the door opening to my cell, soft footsteps approaching my pallet and then the sound of something being placed gently on the floor next to it.

After the unseen person left, I pushed the blindfold above my eyes and beheld perhaps the most astonishing sight of my captivity. On the floor anchored in a puddle of melting wax was a flickering candle next to a heaping bowl of fruit and a big platter with a large "log" type chocolate cake on it. In front of the cake was an intricate, beautiful tiny manger scene. Intricately carved pines stood guarding a tiny wooden barn, open to view at one end. Inside, a minuscule manger was in place before a sitting Mary who held the baby Jesus—with Joseph standing close by. Several shepherds looked on, plus cows, horses, and sheep—all carefully crafted and painted at smaller-than-toy-soldier scale.

I focused my gaze on the baby, who seemed to be looking steadily at some of the shepherds positioned in his line of sight. In the shadowy light of the flickering candle, the moment—like the one almost 2,000 years earlier—was so dramatic and moving for me, I began to feel as if I really were there. The longer this went on, the less isolated, the less constrained I felt.

That mystical moment has stayed with me and continues to influence my life. Today as I struggle to move patiently and I hope inexorably along a servant's path, I realize more clearly that I am simply trying to follow in the shepherds' footsteps and do as they did: testify with my life (as they testified promptly with theirs) about the significance of the great event in which they had played a small part and which I was privileged to recall so vividly on Christmas Eve 1984.

To relate what we witness and try to make sense for others of that long-ago event is what shepherding is all about. It is, I believe, job enough to keep us all meaningfully occupied for the rest of our lives. It is a job with no end, but every day is a new beginning with a new task that I gladly attempt to perform.

44

Mordechai

East Jerusalem, Palestine, December 21, 2004

When you talk with him, he looks straight at you as he gives you his close attention. But his eyes and a significant but unseen part of his being seem to be focused on something in the distance that only he can see. This is Mordechai Vanunu on the verge of celebrating his first Christmas among friends after 18 years in an Israeli maximum-security prison – eleven of them in the lonely and cruel isolation of solitary confinement. He is looking forward to taking part in his first carol sing and midnight mass on Christmas Eve, then a service Christmas morning to be followed by Christmas dinner with all the trimmings.

"My very first Christmas as a Christian was in prison all alone," he says. "I ask the governor of the prison to find a walkman radio for me so I can hear the mass from Bethlehem and he gave it to me."

But where prison coöperation in matters of faith was concerned it was more or less downhill for Mordechai after that.

"I was baptized an Anglican in Sydney, Australia, in August 1986 two months before I was kidnapped by Israel. So my first Christmas as a Christian was in that prison. I wanted a priest and he wanted to come, but they did not give him permission until

January. In all the 18 years in the prison there never was a priest who could come and be with me at Christmastime."

However, the priest was allowed to come on other Sundays. "But for the first five years when the priest came, we were not allowed to talk to each other or to pray out loud with each other. We could only exchange notes. After that I demanded to have a normal meeting, to be able to hear him speak."

Permission was not granted so Mordechai called off the meetings. The silence was too much for him to bear.

"And," Mordechai Vanunu adds, "the prison was happy that I was not seeing the priest anymore."

By Christmastime 1987 sympathizers and supporters on the outside were reaching out to him. "I received books, materials, tapes and people sent me many cards and tapes of Christmas music. I used to hear the mass on the BBC every year from a college in London."

There were still many other episodes by Israeli prison authorities of sophomoric nastiness at Christmastime. "Sometimes they delayed the Christmas cards. They keep them until January," he says without a hint of rancor or bitterness in his voice. "Or," he adds, "sometimes people send me gifts for Christmas, but the prison holds some until January."

The lowest point for Mordechai Vanunu of his entire prison experience was "when they said I am going to be in there 18 years. It was very unacceptable and very unbelievable that I was going to be in that room in isolation for 18 years. But I was. So I fight to keep my spirit free, to keep my mind free. I said from the beginning, they could hold my body, but my spirit and my brain, I will keep free—very free. And that is what I succeeded to do every day."

Mordechai Vanunu was raised in an Orthodox Jewish family, "but at the age of 16 in religious school I started questioning the rules," he says. "There are more than 600 of them and I think that in Israel they cared too much about the rules and not enough about human beings. That's what I thought, because I heard too much that we can cheat for the land. We can fight for the land and we can kill for it."

Years later, after he left Israel to verify and expose its nuclear weapons program to a startled world, he decided to embrace the teachings of Jesus. "Before I went to Sydney, Australia my direction was toward becoming a Christian. Not because I read and knew a lot about it, but because I knew that what Jesus Christ taught was not acceptable for Israel. So in prison I started to find out more about what I have become by reading the New Testament in a very loud voice, to learn it by heart, just like I did for the Old Testament. And I did it for five years, every day for half an hour."

What impressed him most about what he read? "I had already thought that we needed a new way, a new faith, a new understanding of God," he says. "So in prison I used to think about 'Love your enemy.' This is something Israel is not able to accept. They believe in revenge, in fighting and asking God to kill the enemy. But, no, the better way is to love the enemy. That is how we can live together."

Mordechai feels a strong affinity for the Apostle Paul—more of an identification actually. "St. Paul was spreading the message about new ways to worship God and new ways to fight and defend the people. We don't need weapons. We don't need war. We don't need to fight each other. The work of St. Paul was very significant for me because it has been like this in my case also."

Mordechai is asked, "Paul was talking about spreading 'good news,' yet when you talk about the significance and dangers of Israel's secret nuclear weapons program, aren't you spreading bad news?"

"Bad news for those who don't want to make peace," he answers patiently. "Only bad news for those who believe in war or in weapons. The cold war is over. Almost the whole world believes in peace. Only in the Middle East do they believe in war."

How does he equate the Gospel message with what he is trying to do?

"I want to take the nuclear subject, which Israel is still keeping secret inside a very small group, and give it to all people who want to know. I want to take its secrecy out of the dark and bring it into the light. It was in the dark but then I tried to help the light to come. I did it, and I do it, because, if the people have the right to know God and the right to worship, they have the right to know this. It should not be a secret for a super-race or God's chosen people, which is what they call themselves.

"But," he continues, "in this modern age, we are accepting all kinds of human beings: Black, White, Chinese, any race. That is what Jesus Christ succeeded to do. He took the Jewish God from being a super-race and gave it to all of humankind in the whole world. For that reason I am critical of the use of the Bible for politics. In the name of the Bible they came here and took the land from the Palestinians and expelled them. And now they keep them in occupation. Even if they come in the name of the Bible, they should respect the people here and give them their rights."

Despite his release from prison last April, Mordechai Vanunu is not free. He is still more or less restrained by official restrictions and personal apprehension to the only section of Jerusalem in which he feels safe: the heart of Palestinian East Jerusalem where he is living in the guesthouse of the Anglican St. George's Cathedral. Although he has little inclination to go into Jewish West Jerusalem, he is afraid to do it anyway because of the hostility he is sure to encounter there. Walking about East Jerusalem, however, is a pleasure, for he is a respected resident to the many Palestinians who come up to shake his hand enthusiastically or offer a friendly greeting as he proceeds along its streets.

A worrisome moment for him recently was the day of Yassir Arafat's death when, while world media attention was riveted on that story to the exclusion of almost everything else, several carloads of heavily armed Israeli police wearing masks suddenly swooped down on St. George's and swarmed into the compound. Mordechai says, "I was in the dining room eating breakfast. And I thought they are after some Palestinian or running after some criminals. But in fact they are after me. But I am not a criminal. I am not running away. All they have to do is just call me and I will go to them and they can ask me any questions they want. They had a warrant to search my room. I told them, 'Okay. Go search.'"

They took all his materials: tapes, DVDs, notebooks, his computers. And they took him away for ten hours of interrogation before letting him go. Since then all his materials have been returned except the computers. He says, "They are still holding the computers and hope to find something; but there is nothing. I have no more secrets. All I know was published before they kidnap me in 1986."

As far as Mordechai is concerned there is no bad ending to that particular episode. "They can take my computers, but they cannot take my e-mail address," he says with a grin. "I can go to any computer in any internet-cafe and do my e-mails. I can answer my friends all over the world. I am still connected."

If that's the case, does he mind sharing his e-mail address so more people can be in touch? "Yes," he replies emphatically. "I am happy to receive e-mails and to send e-mails. I want to keep connected to all the world, to keep this story alive and to let Israel know they cannot silence me or silence my story. This is a good thing for me to do, because it is an example to other governments that the people in this modern age have much more power now that they are connected. Because of that we can overcome any secrecy."

Merry Christmas and a happier New Year, Mordechai. Or better yet, Merry Christmas and a happier New Year,

vanunumvjc@yahoo.com

[Ed: In the event this e-mail address is changed, contact jlevin0320@yahoo.com].

45

Mordechai Vanunu's Not-so-excellent
Christmas Eve Adventure

East Jerusalem, December 27, 2004

By now some of you already know that Mordechai Vanunu was prevented from celebrating his first Christmas Eve out of captivity in the way he had dreamed about for quite some time: "I was hoping to celebrate my first Christmas out of prison in Bethlehem," he said, "by going with the bishop [Riah Abu El-Assal, Anglican bishop of Jerusalem] for the carol singing when the Anglicans join on Christmas Eve at the Church of Nativity. They go by buses and I was planning on going, too, and then coming back [to East Jerusalem] with them for midnight mass at St. George's Cathedral."

He knew that Israeli authorities would probably consider his defying their restriction against going to the West Bank on Christmas Eve a challenge too difficult to ignore. "But," he acknowledged, "one of the reasons I ran the risk of arrest was because I know it would put Israel government in a very bad spotlight. The world would see that they are just harassing me and not respecting my Christianity, because going to Bethlehem is not about nuclear weapons, it is not about security, it is not about anything except this harassment and not respecting others and their religion – others who are not Jewish. Still, I was hoping that the Israelis would not be so stupid as to arrest me, because I really wanted to go.

"But at around 7:00 P.M.," he said, "the police ring the bishop and told him, 'Don't take Vanunu with you. We are warning you, if you take him, we are searching for him, and we arrest him.' So the bishop says to me, 'I cannot take you with me. They can stop all the buses and stop all the choirs from going on; and we don't want to take that risk to the celebration.'

"So I told him, 'Okay, I will find another way.'"

The bishop wasn't exaggerating the problem his procession of buses might encounter. In his annual Christmas message e-mailed to the faithful and the interested around the world on Christmas day, Bishop Riah reported, "On the way to enter Bethlehem last night our buses were stopped and entered by Israeli soldiers who asked for identification and passports from those who appeared to be Arabs. After being delayed, we were allowed to enter Bethlehem."

Meanwhile, Mordechai did try to find another way. Santa Claus hat in hand, he found a Palestinian who agreed to drive him to Bethlehem. "But before we are even leaving Jerusalem on the road to Bethlehem, the police are searching every car."

Did he feel that the roadblock was set up specifically to check to see if he was in one of the vehicles headed south?

"Yes, and they found what they are waiting for. A policeman recognize me; he check my ID. He sees my name on the ID card, so he speak to his bosses and immediately they decide they are going to take me for questioning."

He was taken to the police station in Jerusalem and from there to Tel Aviv. "In Tel Aviv, I met again the same man who has been questioning me during all those investigations that the police were making against me last month [see chapter 45]. In fact two weeks ago this same man warned me, 'We know you are going to cross the border of Israel to Bethlehem. I'm telling you, don't do it. If you want to do it, ask for permission.'"

Mordechai said that he replied more strongly than he ever had before to the threats, "I am not going to ask for permission. I will go."

He said he spoke more emphatically, "because I don't want to coöperate with their restrictions. To ask for their permission is to coöperate with them, so I said I will not ask it." Then on Thursday, December 23, "I was at the police again for their questioning, and the same man repeated, 'I am warning you, don't go to Bethlehem.'

"But I ignored him. When he comes to talk to me in Tel Aviv at midnight after they arrest me, he says, 'Why? Why you do it?' But I ask him, 'Why you will not want me to go to celebrate Christmas this night in Bethlehem?'

"So he answered me, 'You should respect orders. You are not allowed to go to Bethlehem.'

"But I told him, 'The real situation in Israel is that it exists as an apartheid state. Only because I am Christian there are these restrictions. Otherwise if I am Jewish I am allowed to go anywhere in the occupied territories and for that reason I am not respecting these restrictions.' He was very surprised to hear such news. So I told him more, 'There are checkpoints in Bethlehem where they are checking everyone. They let some to go. Others they do not let to go. There are many Palestinian Christians who are not allowed to go to Bethlehem to celebrate.'

"But," Mordechai continued, "he didn't like that. He didn't believe it. He think Israel is a democracy and all what they are doing is for security. I told him, 'You, Mr. Officer, you make a big mistake tonight. You destroy all your investigation, because all the world is knowing that I was stopped and arrested, because I want to go to Bethlehem; not stopped because of nuclear secrets; not stopped because of security or any other problem, but because I wanted to celebrate Christmas.'"

"And after that?"

"He decide to release me." Mordechai was back at St. George's by about 3:00 A.M. Christmas morning, but there was a "but" attached to the release. Mordechai was put under house arrest at St. George's for five days.

I wanted to know if he felt the bishop should have taken him on the bus despite the police order. With no hesitation Mordechai answered, "I want to tell you this, that he should have been much more courageous, much more firm. He should have said, 'Come with me. We'll take you to Bethlehem. And, if the police will stop us, we will tell them you are just going to Bethlehem to pray and that you will come back with us.' He should not be afraid to take me, because if they stop us and want to arrest me, they can do it. I will go with them. So he should not respect what the police told him, because these orders they are telling to him are not according to human rights, or to democracy, or respecting other religions."

"Did the bishop talk to you on Christmas Day?"

"Yes, we meet but he was laughing and saying, 'Welcome back.' And that he heard about it, but he didn't say much more. He had made up his mind to do it his way."

On Christmas morning the bishop had new problems concerning the harshness and downright duplicity of the occupation to deal with, as reported in his Christmas Day e-mail message. "This morning a pilgrim group was delayed trying to leave New Gate in the Old City of Jerusalem and join us for our Christmas morning Eucharist. Despite all assurances that Christians would be allowed the freedom of worship during this Christmastime, it has not been the case."

I wondered if, in view of the bishop's difficulties in connection with the entire Christmas celebration, wasn't Mordechai's criticism kind of biting the hand that feeds him?

"No, I am not biting the hand that feeds me," he replied quickly. "I don't want to argue with him. He had the right to choose what he wants to do. The bishop has had problems with my case from the beginning and he has tried to be as good as possible. He is also trying to find a way of confronting Israel, because the police are a lot of time calling to him, coming to him, confronting to him, so I have sympathy for him. But I would like him to be more courageous and firm and strong and not fear, because we are not talking about anything that is political involvement or aggressive acts. We are talking about human rights. We are talking about just demanding the basic human rights.

"We should stand firm for our right of freedom of religion – every religion. Israel's Jews are receiving millions of dollars to support and follow their religion. So Christians and Muslims without violence should at least demand their rights to be able to go and pray and worship as they please – as I tried to do. The bishop should be strong, because he is not doing anything bad."

Christmas afternoon, approximately twelve hours after Mordechai's Christmas Eve disappointment ended, a small band of CPTers, colleagues from the American Friends Service Committee East Jerusalem office and a Jewish friend living in Jerusalem came to St. George's, song sheets in hand, so Mordechai got to sing Christmas carols after all, which he did, a little late, but heartily and with a beatific smile on his face.

46

Mordechai and the Double Standard

East Jerusalem, January 8, 2005

Now that our visas have almost expired, Sis and I will be leaving Palestine and Israel for a few weeks. That is more than Mordechai Vanunu can do, hemmed in as he is by official Israeli restrictions, which he ticks off: "Number one: not to leave the country for one year. Number two, if I want to move in Israel, I should report every day to the police where I am going and where I am staying. But I don't want to go into Israel. I want to leave it. Number three: Even though I don't have to report where I am going in Jerusalem, if I want to sleep in another house, even in Jerusalem, I have to report where each night. Number four: I am not allowed to go to the Palestinian territories."

So Palestinian East Jerusalem is "home" for now, and the Anglican St. George's Cathedral guesthouse is his current address. "Number five," he continues, "I'm not allowed to go to any foreign embassy or foreign consul, and I am not allowed to go to the airport."

Then there is: "Number six: not to speak to foreigners like you. Especially the news media. And that," he says scornfully, "is a stupid restriction. Who can know – if you don't see the passport – if you are speaking to a foreigner? I am trying to stand against this restriction. I am trying to tell the authorities they cannot put such a restriction on my talking."

So he doesn't pay any attention to number six. In fact he is surprisingly accessible: willing – in fact, eager – just to chat nonstop or to be intentionally interviewed at length. Anyone who asks (journalists, admiring Israelis, Palestinians, internationals, authors of the humblest of blogs, or members of tour groups serendipitously fortunate enough to come across him as they move about East Jerusalem) are all encouraged warmly to come ahead.

Even though he is available to the news media and the curious, he refuses to speak in Hebrew during interviews or conferences being covered by Israeli news organizations, especially radio and TV. "I am ready to tell my news in Hebrew," he says. "It is very important, because Israeli media are always telling the people a lot of distortions about my story; so I need to correct that. But I don't do it."

"Why not?"

"Because I am ready to forgive but," he admits, "not to forget."

What he can't forget is an acquired wariness based on what he feels is the Israeli news media's long running "distorted" coverage of his kidnapping by the Israeli government in 1986, his subsequent trial and conviction followed by 18 years in prison (most in isolation) and the short leash he has been on since his release last April. Their handling of his story, he asserts, demonstrates how the "Israeli media have used propaganda to develop the minds of the people here to keep quiet about Israel's big secret, its nuclear weapons program, and also not to respect Palestinians. Nothing has changed."

There are those who, although sympathetic with his ideals, courage and long confinement, nevertheless part company with him on this specific issue. His thinking, they worry, is convoluted and counterproductive, a kind of self-imposed Catch-22. By standing the Israeli press in the corner, so to speak, by not speaking Hebrew – especially on TV and radio – he is missing an opportunity to reach out directly to more Israelis.

His answer, "The trouble for me is how can I fight the restrictions? How can I best do that? How can I best express my demand to receive full human rights: my freedom of speech, my freedom of movement? To do that I am giving the Israeli news media, who understand my English very well, a message to get the restrictions lifted. Then I will talk to them in Hebrew."

"But the government makes the restrictions, not the press."

"The media help the government with its propaganda to build the minds and the opinions of the people here. I think the media here are a kind of dictatorship. If the media would help me, that means the state would do it, too."

Failing that, he says, help could come from another quarter but it has not. "I have to fight against these restrictions by myself, alone. But if other states would do something to fight Israel on this not respecting democracy, if they would help me, that would solve the problem."

To do that means solving a series of other Catch-22s, beginning with his desire to jettison his Israeli citizenship. "Six years ago I ask them to take my citizenship and they said you cannot cancel your citizenship unless you have another citizenship. So I tried to find another country to give me a citizenship. I asked even Arafat about five or six months ago for the Palestinian authority to give me citizenship. But the only one to answer was Sweden.

"Sweden said, 'We cannot give you asylum, because you are still in Israel territory. When you are in a foreign territory, then you can ask.' But then some people, who wanted to help me, told the Swedish that I am in East Jerusalem and that East Jerusalem is not part of Israel. It has been annexed; it is foreign country. But that has not convinced Sweden."

He said he also has officially applied to Norway, Ireland, Canada and France and "indirectly to England and to the United States, but no one will even give those who are making indirect approaches for me the papers needed for asking for asylum."

"What's your reaction to all those turn-downs by so many big democracies?"

"It's very sad. The same thing happened during my 18 years in prison. No democratic state demanded my release, so I am used to fighting by myself. And I understand why, even when I don't understand it. No democratic state wants to risk the relationship with Israel for one person. What I don't understand is the world was doing that during the Cold War. All the democracies were fighting Russia for Andrei Sakharov and Natan Sharansky. All of them were fighting this superpower Russia for these two: punishing it, fighting it, making sanctions against it for those two who were doing exactly what I did. When it comes to Israel, no one is ready to fight or punish it for my human rights. It's very strange and unacceptable that the Western states are not doing this for me."

I ask him: "Well, why don't they?"

"It's a double standard by the United States and Europe. The United States has one standard for all the world and one standard for Israel. When it comes to other states, like Arab states, the United States is fighting nuclear proliferation – that is one standard. With Israel, they don't want to know – or see – or speak. They know exactly what's going on. Even more than that, they coöperate. They help each other. So I must keep on asking, How can a democracy have one standard for one state and another standard for another?"

"Is that a rhetorical question?"

"Maybe the answer is: it is a nuclear conspiracy. Maybe it means that states in the West don't want to support a person who is fighting everyone's nuclear weapons, who is continuing to fight alone to report to the world against Israel's nuclear weapons and against foreign governments who are actually helping the Israeli state to keep on doing this. Maybe that is why they don't want me to come to their states, because I continue talking about this nuclear issue."

"Why is it important for us to know as much as we possibly can about Israeli nuclear development?"

"So that Israel cannot play any more games and think that they actually can be allowed to use the atomic bomb. They must be stopped because the atomic bomb is a holocaust weapon that is going to kill children—everyone. It will be genocide."

Are you a one-issue person or is their room for the issue of Palestinian human rights and freedom there?

"My case is one issue. But my story is part of the same issues for Palestine. The same as Israel is doing to Palestine, they did to me. We are suffering from the same government policies.

"So I think Palestinians can learn from how I stand and fight with nonviolence. They can fight with nonviolence too, not by condemning what Israel is doing to them and then doing violence back to Israel, but by standing very firm and demanding their rights, always with nonviolence."

Mordechai Vanunu can be reached by mail at: St. George's Cathedral, 20 Nablus Rd., P.O. Box 19018, East Jerusalem.

47

Mordechai Vanunu's Interview
CONTINUED

East Jerusalem, January 10, 2005

On April 21st, Mordechai Vanunu will have been out of prison for a year, but not out of Israeli custody or jurisdiction. At that time the one-year ban on travel outside the country ends.

Maybe.

Like the administrative detentions of thousands of political prisoners in Israeli prisons–Palestinian and Israeli–his circumscribed conditions outside of jail could be extended. In official (and unofficial) circles, Israelis still feel great resentment toward Mordechai because 19 years ago he lifted the veil of secrecy surrounding Israel's nuclear weapons program. Even though he says he revealed all he knows about the program back in 1986, there is the worry that if allowed to fly the coop, his denials notwithstanding, he will begin sharing as yet unrevealed secrets that will bring activities at Israel's Dimona nuclear facility into a new and still unwelcome glare of international scrutiny.

If that happens, this time the Israeli state probably would not be able to pull off the kind of caper that resulted in his kidnapping, secret trial and long-term incarceration. Like Salman Rushdie, he would probably be well protected from an Israeli-style *fatwa*.

Nevertheless, if all he knows was revealed in 1986, a Vanunu on the outside constantly pointing out the relationship between the Israeli nuclear program and its territorial designs on Palestine could be dangerously infuriating to Israel's land-hungry hawks.

"During the Cold War," he says, "when I saw how many weapons they are producing – more than 100, 200 – I worried that if I do not publish, this very small state, Israel, could use the atomic bomb. I was concerned to prevent that and to contribute to peace by publishing those nuclear secrets."

That concern remains closely linked to the occupation of the West Bank and Gaza. "I make it known to the world that because Israel is so powerful, there is no reason to keep the occupation and not give the Palestinians their rights. That was the real target in my trying to publish about Israel's nuclear weapons."

"If you hadn't gone public, what do you think might have happened?"

"I think the direction was toward Israel to use the atomic bomb. My view is there was a long-time conspiracy to try to use it. After Hiroshima there was no one who used atomic bomb against citizens; and I think some governments were trying to find someone to do it. Israel was ready to use it. So these people think that if Israel do it, all the world will understand, all the world will accept them to do it because of Jewish history. That history, they would say, gives them the right. But then I come out of Israel and prove that just because of their holocaust history they should not have the right to bring holocaust on others."

"You really thought they would use it?"

"Yes, yes. That was the scenario during the Cold War: to start a nuclear war here."

"Here?"

"Yes. There was behind Israel, Christian fundamentalists who want Armageddon here and they tried to have Israel bring it."

"Can all this, if true, be blamed on the Christian right wing?"

"No. But Israel is happy to use them. When Europe Jews came about 150 years ago to this Arab Palestinian region, they say they are a super-race, the Chosen People race and they say the Palestinians are inferiors and not equal. But even more than that superior feeling, the people in the regimes of the Israeli people were believing that they are also in all ways superior to the West, superior to Europe, and superior to the United States. And they still believe it."

"But you also talk about Israeli paranoia. Can there be both?"

"Yes, of course. At the same time, they have this paranoia feeling that the world is against them and they should always be standing against all the world. When they established the Jewish state in 1948 it was after the Second World War, after the Holocaust, the persecution of Jews. Since 1945 the world has been changed and we have many minorities in Europe: Vietnamese, Turkey, Africans and Asian people. There is no such thing as the kind of persecution of the Jewish minority as it used to be in Europe. Israel should understand that in this modern age of democracy and human rights, it is gone."

"But that's not the Israeli official line, is it?"

"No. As you know, I also found out in 1986 they are starting to produce a hydrogen bomb. That is a very strong nuclear bomb. There is no justification of a hydrogen bomb." He adds ruefully, "So if Israelis come to take this land by God, then let God do this for them. Not do it by weapons. They should be destroying their nuclear weapons."

"There are Jews in Israel and elsewhere in the world that are helping you."

"Yes. There are a very small group of them who have supported me. Very, very few."

"There are some Israelis on the left who have been working on your behalf with whom you still have serious disagreements."

"Yes. There are a lot of people from the left who are working for the Palestinians. They are against the wall, against the occupation, but their basic ideology or understanding is not like mine. If these people from the left want peace, they should also accept that the Palestinian refugees have the right to return.

"There are others on the left who are supporting the atomic bomb. Some of them speak of peace, but at the same time they say they want the atomic bomb—like Shimon Peres. They also say they don't like the Palestinian refugees to come back. But if you are for peace, it is contrary to say this."

"But to be fair, there is also a small group of Jews in Israel who are against the atomic bomb and who do support the right of return."

"On the issue of the atomic bomb, you can find some people in Israel who are ready to be antinuclear weapons, but they are afraid to speak because of their work, because of the people around them—their neighbors, their friends who always are telling them, 'Because of the Holocaust, how can you be against the atomic bomb? We are survivors of the Holocaust and now all the Arab world wants to destroy our Jewish community.' So with that pressure they don't say, 'No, we cannot use the atomic bomb.'"

"If you had your way and could go anywhere you want and do what you want, where would you go and what would you do?"

"We have applied for scholarship to MIT or Harvard to be in an academic institution, to do some research in history, to write my book and to spread my message to young students. I want the young students to know and learn from my case. I want them to learn and to know it is important to spread the message of peace, to abolish nuclear weapons and challenge democracies that won't do it. I want to teach them to fight for this kind of freedom.

"Any response from MIT or Harvard?"

"We only made the application in the last month and the application is for the next school year: 2005 September."

"Who is helping?"

"In London we have a big campaign and in the United States, Norway, Sweden, Denmark, everywhere."

"And right now you are still a guest at St. George's?"

"I am staying here [in East Jerusalem] at Anglican Cathedral St. George. I am the guest of the bishop here in the guesthouse. I don't have a lot of expense. People bring me many of the things

I need. Clothes. The guesthouse gives me breakfast. Dinner is the only big expense."

"So that's why you are happy to accept dinner invitations?"

"Yes, but it's also that I am not alone. It is good to have dinner often with friends and journalists who are coming to visit."

"Not everyone knows you have to take care of dinner. Has there ever been an evening when you had no dinner invitation?"

"Yes, of course. Then I go and buy very cheap food–take away. Shawarma or Falafel. I eat it by myself. I could do that for 18 years in prison. I can do that now."

"After 18 years in prison, do you have any resources of your own?"

"I don't have a lot because I spent a lot on the trial and the lawyers. Some people said I should ask money from the newspapers for interviews, but I am not doing that. The campaign in the United States sends me $300 each month. That helps me. And if I can get to MIT or Harvard I have an award of $50,000 from Yoko Ono waiting for me in the United States. So when I can get there, I can start my life with it."

When asked, what if someone wants to help out?–his reply, as always, is unembarrassed and direct, "If people want, they can send directly to me or to the campaign in the United States. I have an account here in Jerusalem."

As my interviews with Mordechai Vanunu came to a close, I decided to end as we began, by seeking one more set of insights into the meaning he has derived from his acquired faith: meanings which drove him, he has said, along the lonely and too often repudiated path of the whistle-blower. Whistle-blower can, of course, be a synonym for Prophet.

"It was the new way of Jesus Christ teachings," he said. "His way of teaching for peace, especially his way of teaching nonviolence. It's hard to understand. It is very hard to follow. I even tried to follow: if they slap you on one side, give to them the other side. That is how people should live in peace: forgive those who are enemies. That is the way we can live together."

Epilogue

Trying to discourage, neutralize, reduce or simply chronicle the aggressive and oppressive violence by the so-called good guys infecting the Middle East (and elsewhere) can be an uneasy and easily demonized calling. Demonizing is what has been happening for decades to any who have become involved. For instance, when Sis and I returned from our Lebanon adventure in 1985 the honeymoon for us with respect to the approval of the political establishment in the U.S. came to an abrupt and unexpected end.

We soon became painfully aware that our understanding of the "futility of violence" context of our rough experience was being sneakily twisted by those who knew better. We could only conclude they were doing so in order to encourage and foment jingoistic hate- and fear-mongering views that were exactly the opposite of what we actually thought and felt.

Because of widespread Western condescending biases and mythmaking masquerading as truth, it was presumed by those who did not really know us that we would agree that what happened to us and the others kidnapped after me was an example of two canards that over the decades have been successfully implanted by Israel-right-or-wrong zealots and their fellow travelers in the U.S. and elsewhere in the world. The first is that *all Arabs are terrorists; Israelis are not.* The second is that the situation is hopeless because everyone knows that *they* (meaning Arabs) *have been fanatically killing Jews for no good reason for thousands of years.*

The fundamental inferences hearers of the above were expected to derive was that throughout history – and certainly now – Arabs have been the aggressors against Jews who have been obliged during all those eons to be continuously on the defensive in a time-immemorial contest against hate and prejudice which automatically entitles the current state of Israel (the so-called good guys) to colonize and establish an exclusivist nation on land which Arabs (the so-called bad guys) have been living for centuries.

Reacting to the shock of hearing those vicious views that were being craftily ascribed to us (until we got wind of them), we began to speak and write out a lot sooner than we had planned which meant the resting up from our ordeal was short-lived. In trying to correct the record – our record – we quickly ran into what I described in an essay that I wrote for the *Washington Report On Middle East Affairs* in 1990 ("Pro-Israeli McCarthyism: When Character Assassination Replaces Political Dialogue" January, p. 47) as *neo-McCarthyism*, a slanderous and libelous condition which equates those who criticize the brutality and territorial aims of the occupation with being *anti-Semitic* if one is not Jewish or of being *self-hating* if one is. Because of my ethical and spiritual evolution, at one time or another I've been charged with being both. Because of my hostage experience I also have been accused of suffering from the Stockholm syndrome.

At the time I wrote the essay I assumed that Israel-right-or-wrong neo-McCarthyism would not last and that there soon would be a turn-around in Palestinian fortunes and the fortunes of the hundreds of thousands of Jews in Israel and elsewhere in the world trying to help Palestine be rid of Israel's colonizing yoke. I have long since stopped harboring such optimistic illusions because the situation since has continued to decline radically for the Palestinians.

Part of this deterioration can be attributed to the neo-McCarthyian political correctness that has escalated to a point in the United States it is now anti-Semitic not to accept, as have both the Republican and Democrat establishments, Bush's semantic metamorphosing of all the settlements in the West Bank (except four very small ones in the north) as well as all those within the dynamically expanding annexed borders of East Jerusalem as sacrosanct Jewish "*population centers.*"

In a real-life exemplification of Orwellian double-think, the true nature of the decades-long squatter movement in the West Bank and East Jerusalem has been verbally eclipsed to the point that it is anti-Semitic if one does not feel obliged to agree that Jewish homesteading has reached such a degree of development and logical permanence that practically speaking there can be no turning back. Thus it continues to be quintessentially anti-Semitic not to accept the political reality of the series of nails that a series of Israeli governments since 1967 (with official U.S. acquiescence and largesse) have been unilaterally pounding into the coffin of Palestinian aspirations.

Ironically the Palestinians' so-called *guilt* or so-called *crime* is to want the same kind of rights we here in the United States, at least in theory, have been considering *self-evident* for more than 200 years. It is also ironic that within Israel's heavily militarized ruling establishment the use of the term *anti-Semitic* has reached such cynical heights when it comes to squelching Jewish anti-militant Zionism colonizing dissent, it has begun to lose some specificity and focus. The use of this expression attained a kind of loony ludicrousness when two Jewish Knesset members accused the leader of a rival Jewish political party of being anti-Semitic. The charges might be laughable except they had little to do with Palestine, but instead were concerned with domestic issues about the concessions every would-be Israeli prime minister must make with religious and secular political parties in order to obtain support for their prospective policies.

Meanwhile, back in the States, Sis and I are still astonished by the number of well-meaning citizens we encounter who don't realize there is no unanimity among either Jews inside Israel or outside with respect to the occupation. However, those who do favor the colonization and support its expansion are well aware of those divisions and often sullenly monitor our presentations which we team up to make to interested audiences around the country.

Often purporting to speak for "Judaism" or "the Jewish people," these interested bystanders try to heckle, refute or undermine our arguments and facts by playing the inevitable What-about-the-*Promised-Land*, *holocaust*, or *suicide-bombers* cards. They usually become angry or surly when I remind them of the thousands of Israeli Jews and Jews from around the world who are horrified, disgusted and disillusioned by the Israeli state's use of those alibis to rationalize its brutal occupation and relentless whittling away of Palestinian (Christian and Muslim) culture, society and polity, while at the same time surrounding what's left with that thick, hard-as-rock, often 29-foot "annexation" wall. Then I show them photos of several nonviolent activists from a variety of Israeli and international organizations hard at work trying to limit, curtail or reverse if possible the dreary, decades-long confiscatory Zionist colonial enterprise–characterized by a series of Israeli governments' relentless intent to forcefully convince the several million Palestinians living in the West Bank to get up and abandon what belongs to them.

Despite Prime Minister Sharon's retreat from Gaza scheduled to take place in the summer of 2005, the colonizing and aggressive unilateral annexation of sections of the West Bank has not slackened since a cease-fire (but not a cessation of settlement building) was agreed to by Ariel Sharon and Yassir Arafat's successor, Mohammad Abbas. The most crucial effect of that cease-fire has been to continue the relentless attempt to transform the Palestinian Authority into a Quisling-like collaboration with respect to security matters.

The success of the unrelenting pressure by both Israel and the United States to turn the Palestinian Authority into prison trustees is giving Israel space and time to achieve a permanent absorption of the more than half of the West Bank it has occupied and expropriated over the years–an area which includes the still expanding areas of East Jerusalem that it has been carving out of the West

Bank which is the half of the pre-1967 West Bank where 99 percent of Israel's persistently growing settlements (*population centers!*) are located. Day in and day out settlers protected by Israeli and police indifference are sallying forth from their fortress towns to harass Palestinian farmers and their families, destroying their crops, poisoning their wells and confiscating more and more of their dwindling productive fields and orchards.

The unvarnished truth about the cease-fires reached in early 2005 is that they are one more example of the sad fact that the struggle on behalf of Palestinian freedom, independence, security and opportunity–opportunity not to prosper but simply to survive–is being lost. If by chance my skepticism is unfounded and the militarized, colonial-minded Israeli political establishment (which includes both Labor and Likud) is as serious as Palestinian leadership is about peace, territorial justice and political parity, we should soon be hearing about Israel turning back to Palestine all the land in the West Bank it has confiscated over the years. I don't suggest holding your breath waiting for that to happen.

So the *piece process* (encouraged and enabled by the U.S.) being masqueraded as a "peace process" continues. As a result, my "From The Inside Looking Out" reports can be expected to continue for –I imagine–quite some time to come. Please stay tuned!

Jerry and Sis Levin are currently based in the Middle East – working at various times in Palestine, Israel, Iraq and Jordan – where they are involved in projects promoting nonviolence as a means for creating a more stable peacemaking environment in the Holy Land and elsewhere. Jerry is a volunteer with the Christian Peacemaker Teams (CPT) working out of their longtime West Bank base in Hebron, while Sis volunteers with West Bank peace-building organizations based in Bethlehem like the Holy Land Trust where she has created a program instructing teachers on how to teach nonviolence and peacemaking. In 2003 the Levins led a delegation into Baghdad as the allied invasion of Iraq began and were there throughout much of the bombings of the Iraqi capital and several weeks of its subsequent occupation.

Jerry was CNN's Middle East bureau chief in Beirut Lebanon in 1984 when he was kidnapped by extremists and became the first of the so-called *forgotten American hostages*. He was able to escape eleven-and-a-half months later due to the efforts of Sis's team of Muslim, Jewish and Christian friends at home and in the Middle East. Dr. Lucille (Sis) Levin is a certified professional mediator who wrote *Beirut Diary* about her successful reconciliation-focused efforts to create the conditions by which Jerry was able to get away safely from his captors.

Jerry shares his ongoing West Bank experiences in internet reports called "From The Inside Looking Out." Those interested in receiving these reports may send their e-mail addresses to jlevin0320@yahoo.com. Sis Levin can be reached by e-mail at drsis2@yahoo.com. Their home base is Birmingham, Alabama. They have five children and eleven grandchildren.

Additional copies of this book may be obtained
from your bookstore
or by contacting
Hope Publishing House
P.O. Box 60008
Pasadena, CA 91116 - U.S.A.
(626) 792-6123 / (800) 326-2671
Fax (626) 792-2121
E-mail: hopepub@sbcglobal.net
www.hope-pub.com